# ainsley
# harriott's
# all new
# meals
## in minutes

| | | | |
|---|---|---|---|
| CLE | | | |
| GCL | 6/06 | HUN | 3/06 |
| GCR | | | |
| GRA | 4/07 | | |
| HUM | 2/07 | MAL | |
| IMM | 12/06 | | |
| LAC | 3/07 | YAH | |
| | | | |

# ainsley harriott's
# all new
# meals
## in minutes

BBC BOOKS

Published by BBC Books, BBC Worldwide Limited,
Woodlands, 80 Wood Lane,
London W12 0TT

First published 2003
Reprinted 2004 (twice), 2005
First published in paperback 2005
Text © Ainsley Harriott 2003
The moral right of the author has been asserted

ISBN 0 563 49321 6

Recipe photographs by Howard Shooter © BBC Worldwide Ltd 2003
Front jacket photograph by Craig Easton © BBC Wordwide Ltd 2003

With thanks to La Cornue of London, Le Papillion Rose, Maxwell & Williams, Muji, Paperchase, and Summerhill & Bishop for the loan of items for photography, and to the following for their help in obtaining the necessary food supplies: Golborne Fisheries, Golborne Road, London; Kingsland Edwardian Butchers, Portobello Road, London; Michanicou Bros., Fruiterers and Greengrocers, Holland Park, London; and Mr Christian's Delicatessen, Elgin Crescent, London.

Recipes developed and written in association with Orla Broderick and Beth Heald

Commissioning Editors: Nicky Ross and Rachel Copus
Project Editor: Rachel Copus
Copy Editor: Kate Quarry
Recipe Analysis: Wendy Doyle
Cover Art Director: Pene Parker
Book Art Director: Sarah Ponder
Designer: Susannah Good
Production Controller: Kenneth McKay
Food Stylist: Beth Heald
Props Stylist: Malika

Set in Humanist
Colour separations and printing by Butler and Tanner Ltd, Frome, England

All the spoon measurements in this book are level unless otherwise stated. A tablespoon is 15 ml; a teaspoon is 5 ml. Follow one set of measurements when preparing any of the recipes. Do not mix metric with imperial. All eggs used in the recipes are medium sized. All vegetables should be peeled unless the recipe says otherwise.

# Contents

# Introduction

Hello and welcome to my *All New Meals in Minutes*. This is my third book in the series and once again I've spoken to lots of people in supermarkets, on the street, in restaurants, and received loads of letters about your likes and dislikes and about how much time you want to spend preparing meals in the kitchen. It's interesting that most of you still want the same things: good tasty food that's healthy and nutritious, the occasional comfort food, handy tips to help you while you cook, recipes that use store-cupboard foods, a little help with menu planning (for everyday meals or a dinner party), not too many ingredients, and you would ideally like to see a picture of what you're cooking. What really is important is that you're not tied to the stove for too long. WHAT ARE YOU LIKE? With that said and done I've set to work with these requests in mind and come up with 80 recipes, each accompanied by a colour photograph – it's always nice to see what the end result will look like.

**low fat!** On the low-fat front this book contains over 20 healthy recipes (each indicated by the 'low fat' symbol) none of which contain more than 12 g of fat. So, if you're trying to watch your weight there are plenty of delicious dishes for you to try without counting the calories, like my *Pomegranate Orange and Mint Salad*, *Lemongrass and Lime Fish Stew* and, for those with a sweet tooth, how about a wicked *Pineapple Ginger and Coconut Sabayon*? I've even included nutritional notes for each recipe, so you can do your own calculations. However, if you fancy something more indulgent like cosy, satisfying comfort food, check out my *Pukka Pea Soup with Crispy Bacon Crème Fraîche*, *Chicken in a Pot with Lemon and Thyme Dumplings* or *Beef Wellington Parcels with Red-wine Jus* to name but a few ideas … and there are some lovely, yummy chocolate desserts.

There are lots of helpful tips and bits of information about different types of equipment that will make your cooking easier and save you time, such as non-stick pans and spring-form cake tins etc. If you're worried about menu planning (i.e. putting dishes together) for kids' meals, brunch, lunch or dinner parties, or maybe even a Thanksgiving Stars and Stripes supper, I've come up with 14 different ideas to help you on your way, which you'll find at the back of the book; there's something for every occasion. It's always nice to get advice on alternatives, too, just in case someone doesn't like a certain ingredient. It can also be fun to experiment with store-cupboard essentials and unfamiliar ingredients, such as buttermilk or fresh raw beetroot and discover new ways to jazz up your meals in minutes. So, I've added lots of variations and alternatives to inspire you in the supermarket, deli or corner shop – and, of course, in the kitchen.

We tend to eat quite a lot of vegetarian food in our house. The *Penne Pecorino and Broad Bean Gratin* is a favourite, as are *Squash and Pine Nut Risotto with Rocket Pesto* and *Chickpea and Spinach Curry with Flat Bread*. It's nice to be able to share these recipes and others with you. There's also a touch of an American influence throughout the book and I'm sure you're going to enjoy my *Chilli and Herb Cajun Cornbread*, *Maryland Crab Cakes with Caper Salsa*, *Pan-fried Chicken with Corncakes* and lots of lovely sweet and savoury muffins.

This time I've included a chapter on drinks, which are always useful to spice up a dinner party, whether it's a *Brilliant Bloody Mary*, an *Apple and Mint Vodka*, a *Peach Bellini* or *The Ultimate Irish Coffee*. In the morning add a fresh dimension to breakfast with a choice of delicious smoothies such as *Honey and Vanilla-bean*, *Banana* or *Berry*, the perfect way to start your day.

I hope you get as much pleasure from *All New Meals in Minutes* as me, my family, and many of my friends do. It's certainly created lots of excitement around meal times.

Enjoy!

# Soups,
# star

# ters
## and snacks

Beetroot borscht • Warm salmon tart • Sour cream and chive muffins • Chickpea and chorizo fritters • Lox on potato pancakes with sweet mustard dressing • Pukka pea soup with crispy bacon crème fraîche • Jimmy's chicken chompers • Mustard-salmon, avocado and watercress salad • Beetroot salad with basil and lemon croutons • Sweet chilli tomato tarte tatin • Smoked mackerel pasta salad with crème fraîche • Mushroom, almond and garlic soup • Pomegranate, orange and mint salad • Roquefort and walnut soufflés • Maryland crab cakes with caper salsa

# Beetroot borscht

Nutrition notes per serving:
calories 113
protein 4 g
carbohydrate 14 g
fat 5 g
saturated fat 1 g
fibre 3 g
added sugar 1 g
salt 1.39 g

Borscht is a general name for a whole variety of Eastern European beetroot soups that vary a great deal. This is my personal favourite as it not only tastes fantastic, but is low in fat and incredibly good for you.

Preparation time: 15 minutes • Cooking time: 45 minutes • Serves 4–6

1 tablespoon olive oil
1 leek, finely chopped
1 celery stick, finely chopped
275 g (10 oz) raw beetroot, peeled and finely grated
1 potato, diced (about 100 g/4 oz in total)

1 carrot, finely grated (about 150 g/5 oz in total)
1.2 litres (2 pints) beef or vegetable stock
2 teaspoons red wine vinegar
1 teaspoon sugar
about 2 tablespoons soured cream
salt and freshly ground black pepper

1  Heat the oil in a large pan and stir-fry the leek and celery for about 2–3 minutes until softened but not coloured, then add the beetroot, potato and most of the carrot, reserving some for garnish.

2  Pour the stock into the pan, season and bring to the boil, then reduce the heat and simmer, stirring occasionally, for about 40 minutes or until the vegetables are completely tender and the soup has thickened slightly.

3  Season the soup to taste, and then stir in the vinegar and sugar. Heat gently until the sugar has dissolved. Ladle the soup into warmed serving bowls and garnish with a small dollop of soured cream and the reserved grated carrot. Serve immediately.

To avoid staining your hands when grating beetroot, use the grating attachment of a food processor or wear rubber gloves.

# Warm salmon tart

Nutrition notes per serving:
calories 549
protein 22 g
carbohydrate 21 g
fat 43 g
saturated fat 21 g
fibre 0.8 g
added sugar none
salt 0.52 g

You can make the pastry case for this tart up to 24 hours in advance, but if you're short on time you can use shop-bought pastry or a ready-made pastry case instead.

Preparation time: 30 minutes • Cooking time: 45 minutes • Serves 4–6

225 g (8 oz) salmon fillet or cutlets
2 eggs, plus 2 egg yolks
150 ml (¼ pint) double cream
2 tablespoons fresh chives, snipped
salt and freshly ground black pepper
lightly dressed fresh green salad, to
   serve (optional)

*For the pastry*
100 g (4 oz) plain flour, plus extra for
   dusting
50 g (2 oz) unsalted butter, chilled and
   cut into cubes
1 egg
1–2 tablespoons ice-cold water

1 To make the pastry, place the flour, a pinch of salt and the butter in a food processor and blend together briefly until the mixture resembles fine breadcrumbs, then tip into a bowl. Separate the egg and set aside the unbeaten egg white. Gently mix the egg yolk into the flour mixture with enough of the ice-cold water so that the pastry just comes together. Knead lightly on a lightly floured surface for a few seconds to give a smooth dough. Wrap in clingfilm and chill for about 10 minutes before rolling (or up to 1 hour if time allows).

2 Roll out the pastry on a lightly floured surface as thinly as possible and use it to line a loose-bottomed 20 cm (8 inch) fluted tin that is about 4 cm (1½ inches) deep. Chill for another 10 minutes to allow the pastry to rest.

3 Pre-heat the oven to 180°C/350°F/Gas 4/fan oven 160°C. Prick the pastry base with a fork, then line with a circle of non-stick baking paper that is first crumpled up to make it easier to handle. Fill with baking beans or dried pulses and bake for about 15 minutes until the case looks 'set', but not coloured. Carefully remove the paper, then brush the inside with the reserved unbeaten egg white to form a seal. Place in the oven for another 5 minutes or until the base is firm to the touch and the sides are lightly coloured.

4 Reduce the oven temperature to 160°C/325°F/Gas 3/fan oven 140°C. Cut the salmon into 2 cm (¾ inch) pieces, discarding all the skin and any bones. Whisk the eggs and yolks in a bowl, beat in the cream and chives and season. Scatter the salmon in the bottom of the pastry case, then pour over the cream mixture. Bake for 20–25 minutes or until the tart is just set but still slightly wobbly in the middle. Serve warm with fresh green salad, if liked.

## VARIATIONS

Why not make double the quantity of pastry and make two pastry cases? Shove one in the freezer and, for a quick supper, defrost and fill with one of the following fillings:

**Stilton and potato:** replace the salmon with 175 g (6 oz) cooked sliced new potatoes and 75 g (3 oz) crumbled Stilton.

**Caramelized onion and goats' cheese:** cook one finely sliced Spanish onion in a little oil and butter for about 30 minutes until caramelized and use to replace the salmon, along with 100 g (4 oz) of crumbled mild, creamy goats' cheese.

**Pancetta and Gruyère:** sauté 175 g (6 oz) of cubed pancetta (smoked streaky bacon lardons) until just golden and sizzling, then use to replace the salmon, along with 75 g (3 oz) finely grated Gruyère.

# low fat! Sour cream and chive muffins

Nutrition notes per serving:
calories 192
protein 4 g
carbohydrate 19 g
fat 11 g
saturated fat 6 g
fibre 0.8 g
added sugar none
salt 0.82 g

These American-style muffins are best served warm. It's nice to use a proper muffin tin, but if you only have an ordinary bun tin this quantity should make about 24 smaller muffins, which cook in about 10–12 minutes.

Preparation time: 20 minutes • Cooking time: 35 minutes • Makes 12

100 g (4 oz) unsalted butter, plus extra
  for greasing
1 bunch salad onions, trimmed and
  finely chopped (about 6 in total)
2 large eggs
120 ml (4 fl oz) cultured buttermilk
175 g (6 oz) carton soured cream and
  chive dip

275 g (10 oz) plain flour
2 teaspoons baking powder
1 teaspoon bicarbonate of soda
½ teaspoon salt
¼ teaspoon coarse-ground black pepper

1  Pre-heat the oven to 200°C/400°F/Gas 6/fan oven 180°C. Generously grease a 12-hole muffin tin, or line it with paper cases. Heat a knob of the butter in a frying-pan and gently stir-fry the salad onions for 2–3 minutes until softened but not coloured. Remove from the heat and leave to cool.

2  Melt the remaining butter in a separate pan or in the microwave. In a separate bowl, beat the eggs, and then stir in the salad onions, melted butter, buttermilk and soured cream and chive dip until well combined.

3  Sift the flour, baking powder, bicarbonate of soda, salt and pepper into a bowl, tipping in any remaining pepper that gets left in the sieve, then repeat to help increase the lightness of the finished muffins. Make a dip in the dry ingredients and pour in the egg mixture. Mix lightly and quickly to combine to a soft batter. Be careful not to over-mix – the batter should be lumpy with specks of flour still visible. Spoon into the muffin tin and bake for 25–30 minutes or until well risen and golden brown.

4  Remove the muffins from the oven and leave to cool in the tin for 5 minutes before transferring to a wire rack (if they are in paper cases remove them from the tins immediately). Pile into a serving basket and serve at once. I love to eat them with some creamy scrambled eggs.

## VARIATIONS

To ring the changes, replace the soured cream and chive dip with another 120 ml
(4 fl oz) buttermilk, then try one of the following suggestions:

**Courgette and Parmesan**: sift 1 teaspoon of dry English mustard with the dry ingredients.
Finely grate a courgette, sprinkle with salt. Set aside for 5 minutes, then squeeze out the
excess liquid and fold into the batter with 25 g (1 oz) of grated Parmesan. Sprinkle a little
more Parmesan over the muffins before baking.

**Mediterranean**: stir 50 g (2 oz) each of chopped sun-dried tomatoes and pitted black olives
into the batter with 1 teaspoon of chopped fresh oregano or a good pinch of dried oregano.

**Breakfast bacon**: grill 6 rindless bacon rashers and, when crisp, chop and fold into the batter.

# Chickpea and chorizo fritters

Nutrition notes per serving:
calories 581
protein 18 g
carbohydrate 37 g
fat 41 g
saturated fat 10 g
fibre 4 g
added sugar none
salt 0.86 g

These fritters are always a winner and are the perfect snack to make when your mates pop round for the footie. The main ingredient is gram (chickpea) flour, which is available from supermarkets, but you'll also find it in health-food shops.

Preparation time: 40 minutes • Cooking time: 20 minutes • Serves 4–6

¼ teaspoon cumin seeds
600 ml (1 pint) milk
25 g (1 oz) unsalted butter
1 red chilli, seeded and finely chopped
1 garlic clove, crushed
150 g (5 oz) gram (chickpea) flour, sifted
2 tablespoons olive oil
1 chorizo sausage, finely diced (about
  100 g/4 oz in total)

1 tablespoon chopped fresh flat-leaf
  parsley,
sunflower oil, for deep-frying
about 50 g (2 oz) polenta or semolina
salt and freshly ground black pepper
soured cream and chive dip, to serve

1 Heat a small frying-pan over a medium heat. Add the cumin seeds and toss and toast for 1 minute until aromatic. Place in a non-stick pan with the milk, butter, chilli and garlic, and bring to the boil. Reduce the heat and slowly add the gram flour, stirring to combine. Cook gently for 5–6 minutes until thickened, beating occasionally with a wooden spatula.

2 Meanwhile, heat the oil in a non-stick frying-pan, tip in the chorizo and fry for a few minutes until sizzling and lightly golden. Pour into the gram flour mixture along with the parsley and mix until well combined. Season to taste.

3 Line a 1.2 litre (2 pint) small roasting tin or ovenproof dish with non-stick baking paper and pour in the fritter mixture, using a plastic spatula. Level the top with the back of a spoon, cover with clingfilm and chill in the freezer for about 20 minutes or until cooled and set (or overnight in the fridge is best, if time allows).

4 Meanwhile, pre-heat a deep-fat fryer or fill a flat-bottomed wok one-third full with sunflower oil and heat to 190°C/375°F. If you don't have a thermometer, the oil should be hot enough so that when a cube of bread is added to the pan, it browns in about 40 seconds. Turn the fritter mixture on to a work surface and peel away the paper. Cut into 7.5 cm (3 inch) squares, then cut in half again, into triangles. Roll in the polenta or semolina to coat. Deep-fry the fritters in batches for 2–3 minutes until golden. Drain on kitchen paper and serve warm with the soured cream and chive dip.

# Lox on potato pancakes with sweet mustard dressing

Nutrition notes per serving:
calories 691
protein 23 g
carbohydrate 32 g
fat 53 g
saturated fat 16 g
fibre 2 g
added sugar 12 g
salt 3.7 g

The word lox, as smoked salmon is known in America, took a bit of getting used to when I first spent time over there. This is an idea I picked up in New York where they love to serve pancakes with just about anything!

Preparation time: 30 minutes • Cooking time: 30 minutes • Serves 4

250 g (9 oz) floury potatoes, cut into chunks, such as King Edward or Desirée
4 tablespoons rice or white wine vinegar
3 tablespoons caster sugar
1 red onion, thinly sliced
2 tablespoons Dijon mustard
3 eggs, separated

120 ml (4 fl oz) sunflower oil
2 tablespoons chopped fresh dill
50 g (2 oz) unsalted butter
2 tablespoons plain flour
4 tablespoons double cream
225 g (8 oz) smoked salmon slices
salt and freshly ground black pepper

1 Place the potatoes in a pan of boiling salted water, cover and simmer for 15–20 minutes until tender. To make the pickled red onions, place the vinegar in a bowl and stir in 2 tablespoons of the sugar and a pinch of salt until they dissolve. Add the onion slices and toss to coat. Cover with clingfilm and set aside for at least 10 minutes (or up to 1 hour if time allows), then drain and keep covered with clingfilm in the fridge until ready to use.

2 To make the dressing, place the mustard in a bowl with the remaining tablespoon of sugar and one of the egg yolks, then whisk to combine. Gradually add the oil, drop by drop to start with and then in a thin continuous steam, whisking constantly, until thickened and smooth. Season and stir in half the dill, then cover and chill until needed.

3 Drain the potatoes and return to the pan for a few minutes to dry. Then, to make a smooth mash, use a potato ricer or, using a wooden spoon, push the potatoes through a sieve set over a bowl. Beat in 25 g (1 oz) of the butter, then fold in the flour and the remaining 2 egg yolks until combined. Slowly add the cream, until you have a smooth batter. Season.

4 Heat a large frying-pan over a gentle heat. Whisk the egg whites in a bowl until soft peaks have formed and fold into the potato mixture. Melt a knob of the remaining butter in the pan and spoon in 6 mounds of the potato mix. Cook gently for 2–3 minutes on each side, turning once or twice until puffed up and golden brown. Keep warm and repeat until you have 12 pancakes in total. Arrange on to warmed serving plates with the smoked salmon on top, then drizzle over the dressing. Stir the remaining dill into the pickled red onion and serve on the side.

For a change, why not serve the potato pancakes with a traditional cooked English breakfast?

# Pukka pea soup with crispy bacon crème fraîche

Nutrition notes per serving:
calories 381
protein 19 g
carbohydrate 16 g
fat 27 g
saturated fat 15 g
fibre 6 g
added sugar 0.5 g
salt 2.98 g

I make this soup all year round as it's perfect to serve chilled as well as hot. It literally takes minutes to prepare and it's funny how you always have a bag of peas in the freezer. The crispy bacon crème fraîche is the perfect finishing touch.

Preparation time: 10 minutes • Cooking time: 15 minutes • Serves 4–6

25 g (1 oz) unsalted butter
1 onion, finely chopped
450 g (1 lb) frozen peas
6 fresh mint leaves, plus extra to garnish
a pinch of sugar
900 ml (1½ pints) chicken or vegetable
  stock

4 rindless streaky bacon rashers
4–6 tablespoons crème fraîche
salt and freshly ground black pepper
warmed foccacia, to serve (optional)

1 Melt the butter in a pan over a medium heat, add the onion and sauté for about 5 minutes until softened but not coloured. Add the peas, mint, sugar and stock, then bring to the boil and season to taste. Reduce the heat and simmer for 2 minutes to allow the flavours to combine, stirring.

2 Meanwhile, pre-heat the grill to medium. Grill the streaky bacon rashers until crisp and lightly golden, turning once. Drain on kitchen paper, leave to cool, then crush into a bowl. Stir in the crème fraîche, reserving a little of the bacon to garnish, and season to taste.

3 Carefully pour the soup into a food processor and blend to a purée, then pour back into the pan; or use a hand-held blender. Check seasoning and re-heat gently.

4 Ladle the soup into warmed serving bowls set on plates. Swirl a tablespoon of the bacon crème fraîche into each one and add a good grinding of black pepper. Garnish with mint and the reserved, crushed bacon. Serve immediately with wedges of the warmed foccacia, if liked.

If you are entertaining, try dusting rings of baby squid in cornflour before deep-frying them until crisp. Add a squeeze of lemon and use as a garnish. They really transform the soup into something quite special.

# Jimmy's chicken chompers

Nutrition notes per serving:
calories 865
protein 41 g
carbohydrate 31 g
fat 65 g
saturated fat 13 g
fibre 1 g
added sugar 1 g
salt 2.82 g

My kids love chicken chompers, and these taste much nicer than shop-bought nuggets. If you haven't got a deep-fat fryer, don't worry, you can still make these as I've included instructions for cooking the chompers in a frying-pan or wok.

Preparation time: 20 minutes • Cooking time: 10 minutes • Serves 4–6

100 g (4 oz) toasted natural
  breadcrumbs
50 g (2 oz) freshly grated Parmesan
4 eggs
25 g (1 oz) plain flour
4 boneless, skinless chicken breasts
  (about 450 g/1 lb in total)

sunflower oil, for deep-frying
a 200 g (7 oz) jar mayonnaise
2 tablespoons sweet chilli sauce
2 teaspoons wholegrain mustard
½ teaspoon clear honey
salt and freshly ground black pepper

1 Place the breadcrumbs and Parmesan in a shallow dish, season and mix well. Break the eggs into a separate shallow dish and lightly whisk to combine. Put the flour on a flat plate and season generously, stirring to combine.

2 Cut the chicken breast fillets into bite-sized chunks, then dust in the seasoned flour, tip into the beaten egg and finally roll in the breadcrumb mixture, making sure at each stage that each piece of chicken is well coated. Repeat with the beaten egg and breadcrumb mixture until each piece of chicken has been double coated. Arrange on a baking sheet and chill for 10 minutes to allow the coating to firm up (or up to 24 hours is fine).

3 Pre-heat a deep-fat fryer or fill a flat-bottomed wok or frying-pan one-third full with sunflower oil and heat to 180°C/350°F. If you don't have a thermometer, the oil should be hot enough so that when a cube of bread is added to the pan, it browns in about 1 minute. To make the dips: place half of the mayonnaise in a small bowl and beat in the sweet chilli sauce and season to taste. Put the rest of the mayonnaise into a separate bowl and stir in the mustard and honey. Season to taste.

4 Deep-fry the chicken chompers in batches for 3–4 minutes until tender and golden brown. Drain on kitchen paper and keep warm until the remainder has been cooked. Pile the chicken chompers on to plates and serve with the dips.

It's easy to make your own breadcrumbs. Simply lay slices of crustless white bread on to a baking sheet in a pre-heated oven at 110°C/225°F/Gas ¼/fan oven 90°C for 25–30 minutes until crisp but not coloured. Transfer to a food processor and blend to fine breadcrumbs – they will keep well in an airtight container for up to 2 weeks.

# Mustard-salmon, avocado and watercress salad

Nutrition notes per serving:
calories 377
protein 21 g
carbohydrate 4 g
fat 31 g
saturated fat 5 g
fibre 3 g
added sugar 3 g
salt 0.71 g

This salad not only looks and tastes fantastic, but is also deceptively easy to make. However, buying good-quality salmon is essential – mass-produced, badly farmed salmon will only give disappointing results.

Preparation time: 20 minutes • Cooking time: 5 minutes • Serves 4

350 g (12 oz) salmon fillet, skinned and trimmed (from a middle cut, if possible)
1 tablespoon runny honey
2 tablespoons wholegrain mustard
2 tablespoons fresh lemon juice

1 tablespoon sesame oil
2 tablespoons sesame seeds
1 ripe, firm large avocado
2 tablespoons extra virgin olive oil
150 g (5 oz) watercress, well picked over
salt and freshly ground black pepper

1 Cut down the middle of the salmon lengthways to give you two strips, then slice these into 1 cm (½ inch) slices. Place the honey in a bowl and add the mustard, half the lemon juice and the sesame oil. Season to taste and mix until well combined, fold in the salmon pieces and set aside for about 5 minutes to allow the flavours to develop.

2 Heat a small frying-pan. Add the sesame seeds and toast for a couple of minutes, tossing occasionally – you won't need any oil as the sesame seeds create enough of their own. Heat a wok or large frying-pan until searing hot. Add a thin film of olive oil, swirling it up the sides, then lay down half of the salmon slices and sear for about 30 seconds.

3 Carefully, turn the salmon slices over, sprinkle over the toasted sesame seeds and cook for another 20 seconds or so until tender, tossing so that each piece becomes well coated in the sesame seeds. Tip on to a plate, then wipe out the pan and repeat with the remaining slices of salmon.

4 Cut the avocado in half and remove the stone, then spoon out the flesh into a large bowl. Add the remaining tablespoon of lemon juice and 1 tablespoon of the olive oil, and then squash with a fork until the avocado is roughly broken down but still has some texture. Season generously, then gently stir in the watercress.To serve, place the avocado and watercress salad in the centre of the plates and top with the slices of sesame salmon.

When choosing salmon, try to select fish that has a bright, glossy colour and firm-looking flesh. I find that Orkney and Shetland produce some of the best fish.

# Beetroot salad with basil and lemon croutons

Nutrition notes per serving:
calories 417
protein 7 g
carbohydrate 29 g
fat 31 g
saturated fat 4 g
fibre 3 g
added sugar none
salt 1.06 g

There are no hard and fast rules for this salad so don't be afraid to play around with a few different ingredients. Experiment with the wide range of goats' cheeses that are now available from your local supermarket or delicatessen.

Preparation time: 15 minutes • Cooking time: 5 minutes • Serves 4

2 thick one-day-old granary bread slices,
  crusts removed
120 ml (4 fl oz) olive oil
finely grated rind and juice of 1 lemon
2 tablespoons balsamic vinegar
400 g (14 oz) cooked beetroot, cut into
  chunky cubes

75 g (3 oz) goats' cheese
50 g (2 oz) sultanas
15 g (½ oz) fresh basil leaves,
  roughly torn
salt and freshly ground black pepper

1 Rip the slices of bread into 1 cm (½ inch) pieces. Heat 3 tablespoons of the oil in a small non-stick frying-pan, add the bread pieces and sprinkle over the lemon rind. Cook over a medium heat for 3 minutes or until they are crisp and have a nutty golden colour. Tip on to kitchen paper and season to taste. Set aside.

2 To make the dressing, place the balsamic vinegar in a screw-topped jar with the lemon juice and remaining olive oil. Season to taste and shake well to combine.

3 To assemble the salad, place the beetroot cubes on a large serving plate then crumble over the goats' cheese, sprinkle the sultanas, croutons and basil leaves on top. Drizzle over the dressing, add a grinding of pepper and serve immediately.

This recipe is a great way to use up any leftover beetroot from the Roasted Balsamic Beetroot (page 144) – it's the reason I came up with the idea!

# Sweet chilli tomato tarte tatin

Nutrition notes per serving:
calories 317
protein 5 g
carbohydrate 28 g
fat 21 g
saturated fat 9 g
fibre 1 g
added sugar 0.5 g
salt 1.31 g

When making any tarte tatin recipe try to use a large, flat plate that is slightly larger than the ovenproof frying-pan. This will enable you to turn out the tarte with much greater ease.

Preparation time: 10 minutes • Cooking time: 35 minutes • Serves 4

3 firm, ripe plum tomatoes
1 tablespoon olive oil
1 small onion, chopped
2 garlic cloves, finely chopped
2 tablespoons tomato purée
3 tablespoons tomato passata
2 tablespoons sweet chilli sauce

25 g (1 oz) unsalted butter
10 fresh basil leaves
225 g (8 oz) ready-rolled puff pastry, thawed if frozen
salt and freshly ground black pepper
lightly dressed green salad, to serve

1 Pre-heat the oven to 220°C/425°F/Gas 7/fan oven 200°C. Cut the tomatoes into slices, then arrange on kitchen paper to absorb some of the excess liquid. Heat a 23 cm (9 inch) non-stick ovenproof frying-pan or skillet. Pour in the olive oil and add the onion and garlic, then fry for about 3 minutes, stirring occasionally, until softened and just starting to brown.

2 Add the tomato purée to the pan with the passata and chilli sauce, then cook over a moderate heat for about 3 minutes until you have achieved a reasonably thick paste. Remove from the heat, season, then tip into a bowl and set aside.

3 Wipe the pan clean and rub with the butter, making sure you go right up the sides. Arrange the tomato slices in a layer to cover the bottom of the pan and place the basil leaves in the gaps. Season to taste, then spread over the reserved tomato paste, being careful not to move the tomato slices or basil.

4 Unroll the pastry and cut into a circle slightly larger than the frying-pan, then carefully place over the layer of tomato paste. Tuck the pastry edges down the sides of the pan, like making a bed! Place in the oven and cook for 10 minutes, then reduce the oven temperature to 200°C/400°F/Gas 6/fan oven 180°C and cook for another 15–20 minutes until the pastry is crisp and golden. Remove from the oven, allow to sit for 1 minute, then invert on to a plate (see introduction). If any tomatoes become loose, simply place them back into the tarte. Cut into wedges and serve with salad.

As an alternative to the sweet chilli tomato topping, you could try serving the tarte with my Chilli Ginger Jam (page 142). Follow the recipe exactly as opposite, but this time substitute the Chilli Ginger Jam for the sweet chilli sauce – great for a change.

# Smoked mackerel pasta salad with crème fraîche

Nutrition notes per serving:
calories 645
protein 22 g
carbohydrate 70 g
fat 33 g
saturated fat 14 g
fibre 3 g
added sugar none
salt 1.36 g

This is a very quick, tasty, simple salad and great for using up any left-over pasta. It also makes a perfect emergency supper. The horseradish works really well with smoked mackerel as it cuts through the richness of the fish.

Preparation time: 15 minutes • Cooking time: 10 minutes • Serves 4

350 g (12 oz) pasta spirals
2 salad onions, trimmed and sliced
200 g (7 oz) peppered smoked mackerel fillets
a 200 ml (7 fl oz) carton crème fraîche or yoghurt

1 tablespoon freshly grated horseradish (from a jar is fine)
juice of 1 lemon
1 tablespoon snipped fresh chives
6 cherry tomatoes, quartered
salt and freshly ground black pepper

1 Plunge the pasta into a large pan of boiling salted water and cook for 8–10 minutes or according to packet instructions, until al dente. Drain and refresh under cold running water. Drain again thoroughly, tip into a large bowl, add the salad onions, and then roughly flake in the mackerel, discarding the skin.

2 To make the dressing, place the crème fraîche or yoghurt in a small bowl and stir in the horseradish, lemon juice and chives. Season to taste. Gently fold into the salad and then stir in the tomatoes. Divide among serving plates and serve at once.

Smoked mackerel is one of my favourites, not only in this recipe, but also flaked into a green salad with my Roasted Balsamic Beetroot (page 144).

# Mushroom, almond and garlic soup

Nutrition notes per serving:
calories 461
protein 8 g
carbohydrate 6 g
fat 42 g
saturated fat 15 g
fibre 3 g
added sugar none
salt 0.55 g

I really like this soup lovely and thick, but if you prefer it thinner, then feel free to add more stock or a good splash of water. It is best to do this after you have blitzed the soup and added the cream as the consistency will alter at this stage.

Preparation time: 10 minutes • Cooking time: 20 minutes • Serves 4

2 tablespoons olive oil, plus extra for drizzling
25 g (1 oz) unsalted butter
1 onion, halved and thinly sliced
3 garlic cloves, crushed
250 g (9 oz) button mushrooms, sliced
150 ml (¼ pint) white wine
300 ml (½ pint) vegetable stock

50 g (2 oz) ground almonds
50 g (2 oz) flaked almonds, toasted
120 ml (4 fl oz) double cream
salt and freshly ground black pepper
a few sprigs of fresh flat-leaf parsley, to garnish
granary bread chunks, to serve (optional)

1 Heat the oil and butter in a large, heavy-based pan. Tip in the onion and garlic and fry gently over a medium heat for 3 minutes until softened but not browned, stirring occasionally.  Add the mushrooms and cook for another 2 minutes, stirring. Pour in the wine, increase the heat and allow the wine to bubble down and reduce for 1 minute.

2 Add the stock to the pan with the ground almonds and half the flaked almonds, reserving the remainder to use as a garnish. Bring to the boil, then reduce the heat and simmer uncovered for 5 minutes, stirring occasionally.

3 Transfer the soup into a food processor and blend to a purée, or use a hand blender, then gradually pour in the cream. Pour the soup back into the pan, season to taste and re-heat gently.

4 Ladle the soup into warmed serving bowls and scatter over the reserved almonds. Drizzle over a teaspoon of olive oil and add a parsley sprig to each bowl. Serve at once with chunks of granary bread on the side, if liked.

Ring the changes when making this soup by varying the kind of mushrooms you use. Chestnut taste good, or you could try mixing two different varieties.

# **low fat!** Pomegranate, orange and mint salad

Nutrition notes per serving:
calories 156
protein 3 g
carbohydrate 24 g
fat 6 g
saturated fat 1 g
fibre 5 g
added sugar none
salt 0.28 g

This salad makes a refreshing starter on a hot day, or serve it as a side salad or between courses as a palate cleanser. Feta cheese would also be a great addition if you want to make it a more substantial meal. So simple, yet delicious …

Preparation time: 20 minutes • Cooking time: none • Serves 4

5–6 large oranges
1 large pomegranate, seeds removed
 and any juices reserved (see tip)
2 tablespoons olive oil

6 tablespoons freshly squeezed orange
 juice
salt and freshly ground black pepper
15 g (½ oz) fresh mint leaves

1  To get lovely slices of orange without any bitter pith, use a sharp knife to take a slice off the bottom and top of the oranges so you can see the juicy flesh, then place on a chopping board and carefully cut away the skin and pith, following the curve of the orange. Cut the fruit into horizontal slices and repeat with the remaining oranges, reserving any juice for the dressing.

2  Arrange the orange slices on a large glass serving plate and sprinkle over the pomegranate seeds. To make the dressing, whisk together the olive oil in a small bowl with the orange juice and any reserved pomegranate juice. Season to taste and drizzle over the salad. Scatter over the mint leaves and serve.

Here's a quick tip for removing pomegranate seeds: cut the fruit in half, use a spoon to scrape out the initial seeds, then turn the fruit inside-out and scrape again.

# Roquefort and walnut soufflés

Nutrition notes per serving:
calories 395
protein 20 g
carbohydrate 9 g
fat 31 g
saturated fat 15 g
fibre 0.5 g
added sugar none
salt 1.52 g

I don't know why people get nervous about making soufflés, because they are one of the easiest and yet most impressive dishes to prepare, so do have a go. You could replace the Roquefort with Gruyère or any of your favourite cheeses.

Preparation time: 15 minutes • Cooking time: 25 minutes • Serves 4

50 g (2 oz) unsalted butter
60 g (2½ oz) freshly grated Parmesan
25 g (1 oz) plain flour
300 ml (½ pint) milk

4 eggs, separated
50 g (2 oz) Roquefort, crumbled
25 g (1 oz) walnuts, roughly chopped
salt and freshly ground black pepper

**1** Pre-heat the oven to 200°C/400°F/Gas 6/ fan oven 180°C. Melt 15 g (½ oz) of the butter in a small pan or in the microwave and use to grease 8 x 120 ml (4 fl oz) ramekins. Sprinkle with some grated Parmesan to lightly coat the bottom and sides, then shake out the excess. Arrange on a baking sheet and set aside.

**2** Melt the remaining butter in a heavy-based pan over a medium heat, stir in the flour and cook for 3 minutes without colouring, then gradually stir in the milk with a wooden spoon and simmer gently for 3–4 minutes until smooth and thickened. Remove from the heat and whisk in the egg yolks one at a time, then stir in the remaining Parmesan with the Roquefort and walnuts. Season to taste, and set aside.

**3** Whisk the egg whites in a large bowl with a pinch of salt until stiff, then beat a couple of tablespoons into the cheese mixture. Using a large metal spoon, fold in the remaining egg whites, being careful not to knock out too much air. Divide among the prepared soufflé dishes, filling each one right to the top and then scraping a knife across the top to ensure an even rise. Bake in the oven for 10–12 minutes until well risen and golden brown – don't be tempted to open the oven door during the cooking time as this may cause the soufflés to flop. Serve immediately.

Nut allergies are increasingly common, so do check with
your guests before you cook this recipe and leave out
the walnuts if necessary.

# Maryland crab cakes with caper salsa

Nutrition notes per serving:
calories 361
protein 21 g
carbohydrate 12 g
fat 25 g
saturated fat 5 g
fibre 2 g
added sugar none
salt 3.54 g

Maryland crab cakes are traditionally coated in breadcrumbs or cornmeal, but this recipe is much simpler. Before you make the patties, have a taste and add a splash more Tabasco or Worcestershire sauce if you think the mixture needs it.

Preparation time: 25 minutes • Cooking time: 12 minutes • Serves 4

350 g (12 oz) fresh white crabmeat, well picked through
1 egg, lightly beaten
2 salad onions, trimmed and thinly sliced
2 tablespoons mayonnaise
1 teaspoon Dijon mustard
2 teaspoons chopped fresh flat-leaf parsley
1 teaspoon chopped fresh thyme, optional
a dash of Worcestershire sauce

a good dash of Tabasco
50 g (2 oz) cream crackers or saltines, crushed

*For the caper salsa*
100 g (4 oz) capers, drained and rinsed
2 ripe tomatoes, seeded and diced
1 tablespoon chopped fresh dill, plus extra sprigs to serve
4 tablespoons olive oil
1 lemon
salt and freshly ground black pepper

1  Pre-heat the oven to 100°C/200°F/Gas ⅓/fan oven 80°C. Place the crab in a large bowl and add the egg, salad onions, mayonnaise, mustard, herbs, Worcestershire sauce, Tabasco and cream crackers or saltines. Mix together with a fork and season to taste. Divide into 12 portions and, using slightly wet hands, form into balls and then flatten slightly into small patties; set aside.

2  To make the salsa, place the capers in a small bowl with the tomatoes, dill and 2 tablespoons of the oil. Finely grate the rind from half of the lemon and stir into the salsa, then cut the lemon in half and squeeze in the juice from one half. Season to taste. Cut the remaining lemon half into 4 wedges and set aside to use as a garnish.

3  Heat 1 tablespoon of oil in a large non-stick frying-pan and cook half the crab cakes for 3 minutes on each side until heated through and lightly golden. Remove from the pan, then drain on kitchen paper and keep warm in the oven. Repeat with the remaining tablespoon of oil and the rest of the crab cakes. Serve with the salsa and garnish with the dill sprigs and lemon wedges.

The crushed cream crackers add a lovely texture to the crab cakes. I find the easiest way to crush them is to put them in a bag and bash them with a rolling pin, or you could blitz them briefly in a food processor.

# Fish and she

# llfish

Buttered salmon and spinach en croûte • Seared tuna with aubergine chutney • Maddie haddock • Mild mustard salmon burgers • Fabulous fish pies with prawns • Spaghetti with clams, pimento and capers • Lemongrass and lime fish stew • Mussels in a thai green curry broth • Smoked haddock kedgeree • Gambas pil pil

# Buttered salmon and spinach en croûte

Nutrition notes per serving:
- calories 1002
- protein 45 g
- carbohydrate 49 g
- fat 71 g
- saturated fat 30 g
- fibre 0.5 g
- added sugar none
- salt 1.53 g

For that special someone or a dinner party these puff-pastry parcels are the perfect main course. Try to make sure the salmon fillets are all about 2.5 cm (1 inch) thick, otherwise the salmon will dry out before the pastry is ready.

Preparation time: 30 minutes • Cooking time: 30 minutes • Serves 4

100 g (4 oz) unsalted butter, softened
2 tablespoons chopped, fresh tarragon
1 tablespoon snipped, fresh chives
1 small garlic clove, crushed
a 500 g (1 lb 2 oz) packet puff pastry,
   thawed if frozen
a little plain flour, for dusting

4 x 175 g (6 oz) salmon fillets, skinned
   and boned (each 2.5 cm/1 inch thick)
50 g (2 oz) baby spinach leaves
a good pinch of freshly grated nutmeg
1 egg, beaten
salt and cracked black pepper
lightly dressed green salad, to serve

1  Pre-heat the oven to 200°C/400°F/Gas 6/fan oven 180°C. Place the butter in a small bowl and beat in the tarragon, chives, garlic, and half a teaspoon each of salt and pepper. Spoon on to a sheet of clingfilm or non-stick baking paper and shape and roll into a cylinder about 2.5 cm (1 inch) thick, then wrap tightly by twisting the ends. Chill in the freezer for about 10 minutes to firm up (or keep in the fridge for up to 48 hours).

2  Cut the pastry into 8 even-sized sections and roll each one out on a lightly floured surface to a 23 cm (9 inch) x 15 cm (6 inch) rectangle, trimming down the edges as necessary. Place the salmon fillets in the centre of 4 of the pastry rectangles. Unwrap the tarragon butter, cut into slices and arrange on top, then cover with the spinach leaves. Season the spinach and add a little nutmeg.

3  Brush the edges of the pastry bases with a little beaten egg and lay a second sheet of pastry on top, pressing down to seal. Crimp the edges all the way round by gently pressing the edge of the pastry with the forefinger of one hand placed between the first two fingers of the other hand, then repeat until you have 4 parcels in total. Using a sharp knife, make light slashes across each parcel, being careful not to cut right through.

4  Place a baking sheet in the pre-heated oven for a few minutes. Meanwhile, brush the pastry parcels with the remaining beaten egg. Transfer to the heated baking sheet and bake for 25–30 minutes or until the pastry is cooked through and golden brown. Serve with a lightly dressed green salad.

You can make these parcels up to 24 hours in advance. If you do, bake them for 30–35 minutes, or until the pastry is golden and cooked through.

# Seared tuna with aubergine chutney

Nutrition notes per serving:
- calories 546
- protein 45 g
- carbohydrate 23 g
- fat 31 g
- saturated fat 6 g
- fibre 3 g
- added sugar 8 g
- salt 0.55 g

In this recipe tuna fillets are seared on the outside but left underdone inside, which is the best way to eat them. A griddle-pan is the perfect utensil for cooking this dish but, if it is sunny, a barbecue would give an even better flavour.

Preparation time: 15 minutes • Cooking time: 30 minutes • Serves 4

about 5 tablespoons olive oil
1 large aubergine, cut into 1 cm (½ inch) dice
1 onion, finely chopped
1 celery stick, finely chopped
a 2.5 cm (1 inch) piece fresh root ginger, peeled and finely chopped
1 teaspoon medium curry powder or curry paste
1 tablespoon tomato purée

2 tablespoons light muscovado sugar
2 tablespoons red wine vinegar
50 g (2 oz) pine nuts
50 g (2 oz) raisins
4 tablespoons chopped fresh coriander
4 x 175 g (6 oz) tuna loin fillets, each at least 2.5 cm (1 inch) thick
salt and freshly ground black pepper
lightly dressed rocket salad, to serve (optional)

1 Heat 4 tablespoons of the oil in a large frying-pan. Add the aubergine, season and sauté over a medium heat for 8–10 minutes until cooked through and tender. Add the onion to the pan with the celery and ginger and cook for another 4–5 minutes or until all the vegetables are softened but not coloured.

2 Add the curry powder or paste to the aubergine mixture, then stir in the tomato purée and cook for 2–3 minutes, stirring frequently. Add the sugar and vinegar with 6 tablespoons of water, give it a good mix, then simmer gently for another 5 minutes until well reduced and thickened.

3 Meanwhile, heat a frying-pan over a medium heat, add the pine nuts and cook for a few minutes until toasted, tossing occasionally. Stir into the aubergine mixture with the raisins and coriander. Season to taste and simmer gently for another couple of minutes to allow the flavours to combine. Transfer to a bowl and set aside at room temperature to cool.

4 To cook the tuna, heat a griddle-pan until searing hot. Season the tuna fillets and smear each one with a little of the remaining oil. Quickly sear for 1–2 minutes on each side until just sealed and lightly charred. Arrange on warmed serving plates with small mounds of the aubergine chutney. Garnish with the rocket salad, to serve, if liked.

Leave any left-over chutney to cool completely, then store in an airtight container for up to 3–4 days in the fridge. It's great with a cheese sandwich!

# Maddie haddock

Nutrition notes per serving:
- calories 448
- protein 40 g
- carbohydrate 8 g
- fat 29 g
- saturated fat 11 g
- fibre 0.7 g
- added sugar none
- salt 1.33 g

This has to be one of the easiest and tastiest dishes I know, second only to my daughter, Maddie, who loves it. The topping is a wonderful store-cupboard standby that's perfect for quick family suppers.

Preparation time: 20 minutes • Cooking time: 10 minutes • Serves 4

2 ripe tomatoes
150 g (5 oz) mature Cheddar
2 salad onions, trimmed and finely
   chopped
4 tablespoons mayonnaise
2 tablespoons plain flour
4 x 150 g (5 oz) haddock fillets, skinned
   and boned

1 tablespoon sunflower oil
a knob of unsalted butter
salt and freshly ground black pepper
boiled new potatoes and lightly dressed
   green salad, to serve

1 Cut the tomatoes in half and remove the seeds, then finely dice the flesh and place in a bowl. Grate in the Cheddar and add the salad onions, then bind with the mayonnaise. Season to taste.

2 Pre-heat the grill to high and heat a large frying-pan. Season the flour and use to dust the haddock fillets lightly. Add the oil and butter to the pan and when the butter starts to sizzle lay in the haddock fillets presentation-side down first. Sear for 2 minutes, then carefully turn over and cook for another 2–3 minutes until almost tender. Transfer to a gratin dish (one large or 4 individual ones are fine).

3 Spread the mayonnaise mixture on top of the fillets, then pop under the grill for about 2–3 minutes until the cheese is bubbling and golden. Serve with boiled new potatoes and a green salad.

To keep the fish moist, cook it until opaque and flaking. To check this, gently prod the thickest part of the fish with a knife and the flakes should separate easily.

# Mild mustard salmon burgers

Nutrition notes per serving:
- calories 429
- protein 34 g
- carbohydrate 27 g
- fat 21 g
- saturated fat 4 g
- fibre 2 g
- added sugar none
- salt 1.98 g

These salmon burgers would work well with any firm fish such as tuna. I like to serve them with my Sweet Eddie Cajun Wedges as the accompanying sun-blushed tomato and soured cream dip works incredibly well in the burgers.

Preparation time: 15 minutes • Cooking time: 10 minutes • Serves 4

550 g (¼ lb) salmon fillet, skinned and boned
2 tablespoons Dijon mustard
2 tablespoons plain flour
4 ciabatta rolls, split in half
1 tablespoon olive oil
a knob of unsalted butter

1 small soft lettuce, separated into leaves
1 small red onion, separated into rings
salt and freshly ground black pepper
Sweet Eddie Cajun Wedges and accompanying dip, to serve (page 134)

1 Using a large, sharp knife, cut away any brown bits from the salmon fillet and discard, then finely chop the salmon. Place in a bowl, stir in the mustard and season to taste. Divide into 4 even-sized portions then, using slightly wet hands, shape into patties. Season the flour and use to dust the patties, shaking off any excess.

2 Pre-heat the grill to medium-high to toast the ciabatta. Heat a large, non-stick frying-pan. Add the oil and butter and, once it starts sizzling, add the salmon burgers. Cook for 2–3 minutes on each side over a medium heat until lightly golden but a touch pink in the centre.

3 Toast the ciabatta rolls under the heated grill. Place the bottoms of the rolls on plates and spread over about a tablespoon of the blushed soured cream and chive dip, and cover with some lettuce and onion rings. Place the burgers on top and smear the tops of the rolls with a little more of the dip. Serve at once with the Cajun wedges and individual serving dishes filled with the rest of the dip.

# Fabulous fish pies
## with prawns

Nutrition notes per serving:
- calories 708
- protein 39 g
- carbohydrate 44 g
- fat 41 g
- saturated fat 24 g
- fibre 3 g
- added sugar none
- salt 0.84 g

We all adore fish pie – it's one of our favourite comfort foods. Experiment with a combination of fish – use smoked haddock or cod and look out for fresh, lightly smoked salmon fillets, which work equally well.

Preparation time: 25 minutes • Cooking time: 30 minutes • Serves 4

1 kg (2¼ lb) floury potatoes, cut into chunks, such as Maris Piper
300 ml (½ pint) milk
150 ml (¼ pint) double cream
1 bay leaf
450 g (1 lb) mixed firm-fleshed fish fillets, such as salmon, monkfish, haddock and cod
85 g (3 oz) unsalted butter, plus extra for greasing

1 small onion, finely chopped
40 g (1½ oz) plain flour
85 ml (3 fl oz) dry white wine
1 leek, trimmed and thinly sliced
2–3 tablespoons chopped fresh mixed herbs, such as flat-leaf parsley, chives and dill
225 g (8 oz) raw tiger prawns, peeled
salt and freshly ground black pepper

1 Put the potatoes into a pan of boiling salted water, cover and simmer for 15–20 minutes or until tender. Put the milk, 120 ml (4 fl oz) of the cream and the bay leaf into a medium frying-pan. Add the fish fillets and poach for 3–5 minutes or until just tender. Transfer to a plate with a fish slice and set aside until cool enough to handle, then flake into bite-sized chunks, discarding any skin and bone. Keep the poaching liquid for the sauce.

2 Melt 25 g (1 oz) of the butter in a pan over a medium heat, add the onion and cook for 4–5 minutes until softened but not coloured, stirring occasionally. Stir the flour in well, followed by the white wine and the reserved poaching liquid; you may need a whisk to help you. Reduce the heat, stir in the leek and simmer gently for 6–8 minutes, stirring occasionally. Add the herbs and prawns and cook for another minute. Season to taste.

3 Pre-heat the grill to medium. Drain the potatoes well, then mash with the remaining butter and cream and season to taste.

4 Lightly butter 4 x 300 ml (½ pint) individual pie dishes. Spread a couple of tablespoons of the prawn sauce over the base, evenly scatter over the poached fish, then spoon the remaining sauce on top. Carefully spread over the mashed potatoes to cover completely and fluff up with a fork. Place the pies under the grill for 5–6 minutes or until the potato is bubbling and golden. Set the pies on serving plates and serve straight away.

You can make the fish pies in advance. When you're ready to eat, simply pre-heat the oven to 180°C/ 350°F/Gas 4/fan oven 160°C and bake them for 20–25 minutes or until heated through and golden.

# **low fat!** Spaghetti with clams, pimento and capers

Nutrition notes per serving:
* calories 475
* protein 16 g
* carbohydrate 78 g
* fat 11 g
* saturated fat 1 g
* fibre 4 g
* added sugar none
* salt 1.86 g

Pimentos, otherwise known as sweet, piquant red peppers, are perfect in this dish. Any leftovers keep in the fridge for up to six weeks, and you could use them to liven up a salad, or drain well on kitchen paper and fill them with hummus.

Preparation time: 15 minutes • Cooking time: 10 minutes • Serves 4

400 g (14 oz) spaghetti
2 tablespoons olive oil
4 salad onions, trimmed and cut into
 2.5 cm (1 in) slices on the diagonal
150 ml (¼ pint) dry white wine
275 g (10 oz) fresh clams, cleaned
 (amande, palourd, telini, if possible, or
 a selection of all three types)

75 g (3 oz) whole pimentos, diced (from
 a jar or can is fine)
finely grated rind and juice of 1 lemon
3 tablespoons capers, rinsed
2 tablespoons chopped, fresh flat-leaf
 parsley
salt and freshly ground black pepper
lemon wedges, to garnish

1 Cook the spaghetti in a large pan of boiling salted water for 8–10 minutes, or as per packet instructions, until al dente.

2 Meanwhile, heat the oil in a large frying- or sauté-pan and gently fry the salad onions for 1 minute. Pour in the wine and allow to bubble up, then tip in the clams and simmer uncovered for 3 minutes or until all the clams have opened. Discard any that do not, as they are not safe to eat.

3 Add the pimentos to the pan with the lemon rind and juice and the capers, stirring to combine. Season to taste; just be careful how much salt you add, as capers can be quite salty.

4 Drain the spaghetti and tip into the pan with the clams and gently stir until combined. Divide among warmed serving bowls and scatter over the parsley. Garnish with the lemon wedges and serve at once.

If your pasta starts to stick once it's cooked, toss through a splash of olive oil.

# **low fat!** Lemongrass and lime fish stew

Nutrition notes per serving:
* calories 219
* protein 34 g
* carbohydrate 5 g
* fat 4 g
* saturated fat 0.6 g
* fibre 1 g
* added sugar 0.2 g
* salt 2.8 g

This dish is beautifully fragrant and I think it is much more refreshing than the traditional hearty fish stews – perfect for a summer evening. If you fancy a change from cod, you can use any firm-fleshed white fish for this recipe.

Preparation time: 20 minutes • Cooking time: 12 minutes • Serves 4

1 tablespoon sunflower oil
8 salad onions, trimmed and sliced
2 garlic cloves, crushed
a 5 cm (2 inch) piece fresh root ginger, finely grated
2 lemongrass stalks, outer leaves removed and the core finely chopped
1 red chilli, seeds removed and finely diced
150 ml (¼ pint) dry white wine

600 ml (1 pint) fresh fish stock (from a carton is fine)
finely grated rind and juice of 2 limes
750 g (1½ lb) cod, skinned and cut into 2.5 cm (1 inch) cubes
150 g (5 oz) mangetout, shredded
3 tablespoons Thai fish sauce (nam pla)
a good handful of fresh coriander sprigs, to garnish

1 Heat the oil in a large, heavy-based pan and fry the salad onions for 2 minutes. Add the garlic, ginger, lemongrass and chilli, then continue to cook over a low heat for another 2 minutes, stirring.

2 Add the wine to the pan, increase the heat and allow to reduce for 3 minutes, then pour in the stock and lime juice and bring to a gentle simmer. Add the fish and simmer uncovered for 3 minutes or until the fish is tender but still holding its shape.

3 Add the mangetout to the pan and cook for another 2 minutes until tender. Stir in the fish sauce and ladle into warmed, wide-rimmed serving bowls. Garnish with lime rind and coriander sprigs. Serve at once.

If you are short of time, try using the jars of chopped garlic, chilli, lemongrass and ginger that are available in supermarkets. You'll need 1 teaspoon each of garlic and chilli and 2 teaspoons each of ginger and lemongrass.

Fresh fish stock is now available in cartons in all
supermarkets. You could, of course, make your own,
but I never usually bother.

# Mussels in a thai green curry broth

This is a delicious, delicately fragrant dish that has the added bonus of being two meals in one; first you eat the mussels and then finish with the soup. I find that half a mussel shell makes the perfect spoon!

Nutrition notes per serving:
calories 194
protein 12 g
carbohydrate 6 g
fat 14 g
saturated fat 11 g
fibre 0.2 g
added sugar 0.1 g
salt 2.19 g

Preparation time: 15 minutes • Cooking time: 15 minutes • Serves 4

15 g (½ oz) bunch fresh coriander
2 cm (¾ inch) fresh root ginger, finely chopped
1 lemongrass stalk, outer leaves removed and the core finely chopped
grated rind and juice of 1 lime
1 tablespoon Thai fish sauce (nam pla) or light soy sauce
2 green chillies, thinly sliced

2 garlic cloves, crushed
2 salad onions, thinly sliced
1 teaspoon cumin seeds, crushed
1 tablespoon sunflower oil
600 ml (1 pint) fresh fish stock
300 ml (½ pint) coconut milk
1 kg (2¼ lb) fresh mussels, cleaned
salt and freshly ground black pepper

1  Remove a good handful of the coriander leaves from the stalks for garnish and set aside. Roughly chop the remainder, including the stalks, and place in a mini blender with the ginger, lemongrass, lime rind and juice, Thai fish sauce or soy, chillies, garlic, salad onions and cumin. Whizz to a paste or, if you don't have a mini blender, use a pestle and mortar or very finely chop with a large knife.

2  Heat the oil in a large pan with a lid and add the paste, cook for 1 minute, stirring. Pour in the stock and coconut milk and bring up to the boil, then reduce the heat and simmer for 5 minutes until fragrant. Season generously.

3  Add the mussels to the pan, cover tightly and cook for 3–4 minutes, shaking the pan halfway through. All the mussels should now have opened – discard any that do not. Ladle the mussels and broth into large serving bowls and garnish with the reserved coriander leaves to serve.

# Smoked haddock kedgeree

The basis of this dish dates from Victorian times, when the leftover rice and fish from the previous evening's meal were mixed together with butter and served for breakfast. However, for me, cooking it from scratch appeals much more.

Preparation time: 5 minutes • Cooking time: 20 minutes • Serves 4

350 g (12 oz) undyed smoked haddock
2 eggs
2 tablespoons olive oil
½ teaspoon cumin seeds
1 teaspoon medium curry powder
225 g (8 oz) basmati rice
2 tablespoons sultanas
50 g (2 oz) unsalted butter
1 small onion, finely chopped

5 cm (2 inch) fresh root ginger, finely grated
1 teaspoon ground turmeric
½ teaspoon tomato purée
150 ml (¼ pint) double cream
2 tablespoons chopped fresh flat-leaf parsley
salt and freshly ground black pepper

1 Place the haddock in a small sauté pan and cover with cold water. Bring to a simmer, and cook uncovered for 3–4 minutes. Drain, reserving 3 tablespoons of the poaching liquid to add to the sauce. Allow the haddock to cool a little, then flake into bite-sized pieces, discarding any skin and bone. Boil the eggs in a small pan for 7–8 minutes (3–4 minutes longer if you like them really hard-boiled). Drain, run under cold running water, remove the shell, then chop.

2 Heat the oil in a large pan, then add the cumin seeds and curry powder and cook over a high heat for 1 minute, stirring. Tip in the rice and sultanas and continue to cook for another minute, stirring. Pour in 900 ml (1½ pints) of water and bring to the boil, then boil steadily for 10 minutes until tender.

3 Meanwhile, make the sauce. Melt the butter in a frying-pan and sauté the onion, ginger and turmeric over a medium heat for 2 minutes until softened but not browned. Stir in the tomato purée and cook for another 2 minutes, stirring. Pour in the cream and simmer for 3 minutes, then stir in the parsley and reserved poaching liquid to just heat through. Season to taste.

4 Use a fork to fluff up the cooked rice and then gently fold in the flaked haddock. Divide among warmed serving plates and drizzle over the sauce. Garnish with the chopped, hard-boiled eggs and serve immediately.

I always recommend buying undyed smoked haddock, rather than the artificial bright-yellow-coloured type.

Nutrition notes per serving:
- calories 657
- protein 63 g
- carbohydrate 3 g
- fat 44 g
- saturated fat 26 g
- fibre 0.3 g
- added sugar none
- salt 1.96 g

# Gambas pil pil

The first time I had this was on a beach in Spain with the sand between my toes, where the hot sun kept the butter bubbling for longer. If possible, use fresh prawns, but take off the shells before cooking as otherwise it gets a bit messy.

Preparation time: 10 minutes • Cooking time: 6 minutes • Serves 4

300 g (10 oz) unsalted butter
3 garlic cloves, crushed
1 tablespoon smoked paprika
1.5 kg (3 lb) raw tiger prawns, peeled and veins removed, but tails intact (64–80 in total)
2 tablespoons chopped fresh flat-leaf parsley
salt and freshly ground black pepper
lemon wedges, to garnish
fresh crusty bread, to serve

1 Melt the butter in a pan with the garlic and paprika and season generously. When the butter is just starting to foam, tip in the prawns – stand back as they may spit. Cook the prawns for 2–3 minutes or until they have changed to a pinky-orange colour and are tender and cooked through.

2 Spoon the prawns and butter mixture into serving bowls and scatter over the parsley. Garnish with the lemon wedges and serve at once with plenty of crusty bread. You may like to have a finger bowl or some napkins at the ready!

The paprika you use in this dish makes all the difference.
Wonderful smoked paprika is now available in larger
supermarkets; you'll find it in the gourmet foods area.

# Quick
# pou

# and delicious
# poultry

Calypso pepperpot chicken with plantain ● Honey-glazed duck with sticky rice ● Chicken and sun-blushed tomato salad ● Roasted chicken breast with courgette stuffing ● Pan-fried chicken with corncakes ● Chicken in a pot with lemon and thyme dumplings ● Aromatic pad thai chicken ● Crispy chilli orange grilled chicken ● Flambé tequila chicken with pine nuts ● Tempting turkey, leek and mushroom pies

# Calypso pepperpot chicken with plantain

Nutrition notes per serving:
★ calories 554
★ protein 37 g
★ carbohydrate 22 g
★ fat 36 g
★ saturated fat 22 g
★ fibre 2 g
★ added sugar none
★ salt 0.63 g

If you can't stand the heat, get out of the kitchen and cook on a barbie, or if the sun doesn't shine a griddle pan works fine, 'cos it's Calypso Pepperpot Chicken time. You can marinate the chicken overnight; just cover with clingfilm and refrigerate.

Preparation time: 20 minutes • Cooking time: 20 minutes • Serves 4

3 teaspoons West Indian hot pepper
  sauce
2 garlic cloves, crushed
1 teaspoon paprika
1 teaspoon dried thyme
2 tablespoons chopped fresh coriander,
  plus sprigs for the garnish
3 tablespoons olive oil

4 boneless, skinless chicken breasts
a 200 ml (7 fl oz) carton coconut cream
1 small ripe mango, peeled, stoned and
  diced (about 175 g/6 oz in total)
juice of ½ lime
2 large, ripe plantains
40 g (1½ oz) unsalted butter
salt and cracked black pepper

1 Place 2 teaspoons of the pepper sauce in a shallow non-metallic dish with the garlic, paprika, thyme, half the coriander, half a teaspoon of salt and 2 teaspoons of cracked black pepper; add the oil and stir until well combined. Lightly slash each chicken breast and then rub in the pepper mixture until well coated.

2 Pre-heat the grill to medium. Arrange the chicken breasts on the grill rack and cook for 6–8 minutes on each side until the chicken is cooked through and lightly charred.

3 Place the coconut cream and mango pieces in a pan and bring to the boil, then reduce the heat and simmer gently for about 5 minutes or until the mango is tender. Add the remaining teaspoon of pepper sauce, 1 tablespoon chopped coriander and the lime juice, then blend to a purée in a food processor or with a hand blender. Season to taste with pepper and transfer to a bowl.

4 Peel the plantain and cut each one across into two pieces, then cut each piece in half, lengthways. Heat a large frying-pan and melt the butter, add the plantain pieces and fry over a medium-high heat for about 2 minutes on each side until lightly golden. Drain on kitchen paper.

5 To serve, arrange the plantain pieces on plates with the calypso chicken. Divide the coconut sauce between individual dishes and place on the side of each plate. Serve at once.

Plantains belong to the banana family. They are ready to use when the skins begin to go black, like an over-ripe banana.

# Honey-glazed duck
## with sticky rice

Nutrition notes per serving:
★ calories 743
★ protein 37 g
★ carbohydrate 65 g
★ fat 39 g
★ saturated fat 10 g
★ fibre 1.75 g
★ added sugar 9 g
★ salt 2.48 g

I love duck and this has to be one of my favourite ways of cooking it. Obviously the longer you can leave it in the marinade the better – up to 24 hours is fine, covered with clingfilm in the fridge.

Preparation time: 25 minutes • Cooking time: 20 minutes • Serves 4

3 tablespoons clear honey
3 tablespoons dark soy sauce
juice and finely grated rind of 1 small
   orange
2 tablespoons sesame seeds
4 x 175–200 g (6–7 oz) skin-on duck
   breasts

275 g (10 oz) sushi rice
a pinch of salt
120 ml (4 fl oz) chicken stock
fresh coriander leaves and shredded
   salad onions, to garnish
Wok-style Pak Choi, to serve (page 130)

1  Pre-heat the oven to 200°C/400°F/Gas 6/fan oven 180°C. Place the honey in a shallow, non-metallic dish and add the soy sauce, orange juice and rind and sesame seeds, stirring to combine. Add the duck, turning to coat, and set aside at room temperature for 15 minutes, turning occasionally.

2  To make the sticky rice, rinse the rice thoroughly under cold running water and place in a pan with 600 ml (1 pint) of cold water. Add the salt and bring to the boil, then stir once. Reduce the heat, cover and simmer for 8 minutes until all the water is completely absorbed. Turn off the heat and leave the rice to steam for at least another 4–6 minutes until tender – it should sit happily for up to 20 minutes with the lid on.

3  Heat a large, ovenproof frying-pan until searing hot. Drain the marinade from the duck and reserve, then add the duck to the heated pan skin-side down and quickly seal, making sure the skin is slightly blackened. Turn over and just seal, then transfer to the oven and roast for 8–10 minutes until just tender but still slightly pink in the middle. If you prefer your duck more well done, give it another 2–3 minutes.

4  Tip the remaining marinade into a small pan with the stock and bring to the boil, then reduce the heat and simmer gently for 3–4 minutes until reduced to a sauce consistency, stirring occasionally. Remove the duck from the oven and leave to rest for about 5 minutes in a warm place, then carve on the diagonal. Spoon the rice into warmed serving bowls and arrange the duck on top, then drizzle around the reduced sauce. Garnish with the coriander leaves and salad onions. Serve with the Wok-style Pak Choi.

Sushi rice is available in Asian stores and good supermarkets, but if you can't get hold of it I would suggest a fragrant rice such as Thai or basmati.

# Chicken and sun-blushed tomato salad

Nutrition notes per serving:
★ calories 353
★ protein 30 g
★ carbohydrate 11 g
★ fat 21 g
★ saturated fat 3 g
★ fibre 1 g
★ added sugar 2 g
★ salt 2.53 g

Fragrant chicken and olives, salad leaves and succulent sun-blushed tomatoes make up this tempting salad. To make it more substantial, add steamed baby new potatoes, halved and tossed in a little dressing while they are still warm.

Preparation time: 25 minutes • Cooking time: 5 minutes • Serves 4

2 teaspoons garam masala
¼ teaspoon paprika
¼ teaspoon ground cumin
1 teaspoon mild chilli powder
1 garlic clove, crushed
juice of 1 lime
6 tablespoons olive oil
4 boneless, skinless chicken breasts
  (about 450 g/1 lb in total)

2 teaspoons clear honey
a 200 g (7 oz) bag Italian-style salad
100 g (4 oz) sun-blushed tomatoes
  (see tip)
100 g (4 oz) black olives, pitted (good
  quality, such as Kalamata)
salt and cracked black pepper
ciabatta bread, to serve, optional

1 Place the garam masala in a shallow, non-metallic dish with the paprika, cumin, chilli powder, garlic, half the lime juice, half a teaspoon each of salt and pepper and 2 tablespoons of the olive oil. Stir to combine. Cut the chicken breasts into 2 cm (¾ inch) strips and toss in the spice mixture until well coated. Set aside for at least 15 minutes to allow the flavours to develop (or up to 24 hours is fine, covered with clingfilm in the fridge).

2 Heat a large, non-stick frying-pan over a medium heat and then add the chicken strips. Cook for about 2 minutes on each side until cooked through and well seared.

3 Place the remaining lime juice and the honey in a screw-topped jar. Season to taste, then shake vigorously until the salt has dissolved. Add the remaining 4 tablespoons of olive oil and shake again until emulsified.

4 Tip the salad leaves into a bowl with the sun-blushed tomatoes and olives. Add enough of the dressing to just barely coat the leaves. Divide between serving plates and arrange the seared chicken pieces on top. Serve at once with chunks of ciabatta bread, if liked.

Sun-blushed tomatoes are semi sun-dried and need no soaking. You'll find them in supermarkets on the deli counter, or in the chilled section.

If time allows, leave the stuffed chicken breast to firm up in the fridge for an hour or two. This will ensure that no stuffing bursts out during cooking.

# Roasted chicken breast
## with courgette stuffing

If you fancy a spot of gravy with this dish, simply stir a tablespoon of plain flour into the cooking juices, then gradually add 120 ml (4 fl oz) of chicken stock, whisking to combine. Simmer for a couple of minutes, sieve and serve.

Preparation time: 30 minutes • Cooking time: 40 minutes • Serves 4

2 courgettes (about 225 g/8 oz in total)
40 g (1½ oz) unsalted butter, at room temperature
1 small onion, finely chopped
50 g (2 oz) full-fat soft cheese
25 g (1 oz) fine white breadcrumbs, made from day-old bread
1 egg yolk

2 tablespoons chopped fresh mixed herbs (such as tarragon, parsley and chervil)
2 tablespoons freshly grated Parmesan
4 large boneless, skin-on chicken breasts
1 tablespoon olive oil
salt and freshly ground black pepper
roasted new potatoes, to serve

1  Pre-heat the oven to 200°C/400°F/Gas 6/fan oven 180°C. Top and tail the courgettes, then coarsely grate in a food processor, or use a mandolin or box grater. Tip into a clean tea towel and squeeze out any excess moisture.

2  Melt a knob of the butter in a large, ovenproof frying-pan. Add the onion and cook for 2–3 minutes until softened but not browned. Add the grated courgettes, increase the heat and sauté for another 3–4 minutes until just tender. Tip on to a plate to cool a little.

3  Using a fork, soften the remaining butter in a bowl, then beat in the soft cheese. Mix in half the breadcrumbs, the egg yolk, herbs, and onion and courgette mixture, mixing well to combine. Stir in the remaining breadcrumbs and Parmesan, and then season to taste.

4  Wipe out the frying-pan and return to the heat. Using a sharp knife, make a pocket in each chicken breast by cutting horizontally almost all the way through but leaving them attached at one side, then push about a tablespoon of the stuffing into each, spreading it with a round-bladed knife. Carefully lift the skin of each breast and spread a little more of the stuffing between the flesh and the skin, then seal and secure with cocktail sticks. Season all over.

5  Add the olive oil to the frying-pan, then cook the chicken breasts skin-side down for 3–4 minutes, until golden, turning once. Transfer to the oven and cook for another 15–20 minutes or until cooked through. Remove from the oven, and leave to rest for 5 minutes. Carve each chicken breast into 3 slices and arrange on warmed serving plates accompanied by roasted new potatoes.

# Pan-fried chicken
## with corncakes

Nutrition notes per serving:
★ calories 624
★ protein 25 g
★ carbohydrate 61 g
★ fat 33 g
★ saturated fat 3 g
★ fibre 2 g
★ added sugar 12 g
★ salt 2 g

Corn- or maize-fed chickens have a distinctive colour, and marinating them in buttermilk helps retain their delicious moistness. I've used the rest of the buttermilk to make corncakes – great with the chicken and a tangy sauce.

Preparation time: 25 minutes • Cooking time: 30 minutes • Serves 4

120 ml (4 fl oz) cultured buttermilk
2 garlic cloves, crushed
4 x 75 g (3 oz) boneless chicken breasts
   (corn-fed, if possible)
1 teaspoon cayenne pepper
100 g (4 oz) self-raising flour
sunflower oil, for frying
50 g (2 oz) cornflour
2 eggs, beaten

4 salad onions, finely chopped
1 tablespoon chopped fresh flat-leaf
   parsley, plus extra to garnish
a 325 g (10½ oz) can sweetcorn kernels,
   drained and rinsed
salt and cracked black pepper
shop-bought ranchero or chunky
   barbecue sauce, to serve

1 Place the buttermilk in a bowl with the garlic, season and add the chicken, turning to coat. Set aside for 5 minutes.

2 In a bowl or plastic bag, combine the cayenne pepper with 4 tablespoons of the flour and 1 teaspoon each of salt and pepper. One by one, lift the chicken breasts out of the buttermilk, shaking off any excess, and dip into the flour mixture to coat evenly, again shaking off any excess. Reserve the remaining buttermilk mixture.

3 Heat a 5 mm (¼ inch) layer of oil in a large frying-pan. Add the chicken, skin-side down, and cook for 8 minutes until the skin is crisp and browned. Turn the chicken over and cook for another 2–3 minutes until golden. Drain on kitchen paper and transfer to a warm plate.

4 Sieve the remaining flour and the cornflour into a bowl with half a teaspoon of salt and 1 teaspoon of pepper. Make a well in the centre and pour in the eggs and 6 tablespoons of the reserved buttermilk mixture. Beat until smooth. Stir in the salad onions, parsley and sweetcorn. Place a large, non-stick frying-pan over a medium heat, add 2 tablespoons of oil and swirl around until heated, then spoon in ladlefuls of the batter – you'll need 8 corncakes in total so, depending on the size of your pan, you may need to do them in batches. Cook for 3–4 minutes on each side until crisp and lightly golden. Drain on kitchen paper. Place 2 corncakes on each warmed serving plate. Place the rested chicken on top. Serve with a separate bowl of ranchero or barbecue sauce.

Fried chicken is very much a tradition in the southern states of America, where it is served with bread rolls spread with lots of butter.

# Chicken in a pot with lemon and thyme dumplings

Nutrition notes per serving:
★ calories 496
★ protein 35 g
★ carbohydrate 43 g
★ fat 19 g
★ saturated fat 6 g
★ fibre 7 g
★ added sugar none
★ salt 1.73 g

When you're in the mood for a real winter warmer that has loads of flavour, appeals to all the family and takes little time to prepare compared to traditional casseroles, you can't go far wrong with this delicious one-pot supper.

Preparation time: 15 minutes • Cooking time: 30 minutes • Serves 4

2 tablespoons olive oil
3 boneless, skinless chicken breasts, cut into strips
1 onion, sliced
2 garlic cloves, crushed
2 carrots, cut into chunky slices
2 leeks, well trimmed and sliced
120 ml (4 fl oz) white wine
3 fresh thyme sprigs
900 ml (1½ pints) chicken stock

a 400 g (14 oz) can cannellini beans, drained and rinsed
*For the dumplings*
100 g (4 oz) plain flour, plus a little extra for dusting
1 teaspoon baking powder
2 teaspoons chopped fresh thyme leaves
grated rind of 1 lemon
50 g (2 oz) shredded suet
salt and freshly ground black pepper

1 Heat the oil in a large pan with a lid. Add the chicken, season generously and cook on a fairly high heat for 2 minutes until browned and sealed all over. Add the onion and garlic and continue to fry for another 2 minutes until the onion has softened slightly but not coloured, stirring occasionally.

2 Tip the carrots and leeks into the pan, then pour in the wine and add the thyme, allowing the wine to reduce for 1 minute over a high heat. Stir in the stock and then simmer for 10 minutes until the vegetables are tender and the liquid has slightly reduced. Season to taste.

3 Meanwhile, make the dumplings. Place the flour in a bowl and add the baking powder, thyme, lemon rind and a pinch of salt. Stir in the suet and then gradually add 120 ml (4 fl oz) of cold water until the mixture forms a soft dough. Divide the dough into 8 then, using lightly floured hands, shape into balls.

4 Stir the cannellini beans into the casserole and then sit the dumplings on the top. Cover and simmer for another 10 minutes until the dumplings have slightly puffed up and cooked through. Check the seasoning. To serve, ladle the chicken into warmed serving bowls and top with a couple of dumplings.

Why not let the kids help out with this recipe? Mine love to get involved by shaping the dumplings.

# low fat! Aromatic pad thai chicken

Nutrition notes per serving:
- calories 402
- protein 22 g
- carbohydrate 55 g
- fat 12 g
- saturated fat 2 g
- fibre 0.1 g
- added sugar 0.5 g
- salt 3.66 g

The best pad Thai I have ever eaten was sitting on a very small rickety chair on the pavement in Bangkok. The aroma was sensational with the combination of all those wonderful ingredients.

Preparation time: 15 minutes • Cooking time: 15 minutes • Serves 4

250 g (9 oz) thick dried flat rice noodles
2 tablespoons sunflower oil
2 boneless, skinless chicken breasts, cut into 2 cm (¾ inch) strips
1 shallot, finely sliced
2.5 cm (1 inch) fresh root ginger or galangal, finely chopped
1 lemongrass stalk, outer leaves removed and the core finely chopped
1 red bird's-eye chilli, seeded and finely chopped

2 kaffir lime leaves, finely shredded
1 garlic clove, finely chopped
4 baby pak choi or bok choy, quartered
3 tablespoons dark soy sauce
2 tablespoons Thai fish sauce (nam pla)
2 fresh limes
2 tablespoons sesame oil
3 tablespoons chopped, roasted peanuts (optional)
a large handful of fresh coriander leaves, to garnish

1 Soak the noodles in a large bowl of boiling water for 6 minutes or as per the packet instructions. Heat the oil in a large wok or frying-pan and stir-fry the chicken over a medium heat for 4–5 minutes until just starting to brown.

2 Add the shallot to the wok with the ginger or galangal, lemongrass, chilli, lime leaves and garlic, stirring to combine, then tip in the pak choi or bok choy and stir-fry for another 2 minutes.

3 Pour the soy and fish sauce into the wok and simmer for 4 minutes until the chicken is cooked through and tender. Squeeze over the juice of 1 lime and stir to combine.

4 Drain the noodles and tip into the chicken, then toss and stir until well combined. Divide the pad Thai among warmed serving bowls, drizzle over a little sesame oil, a scattering of peanuts, if using, and a few sprigs of fresh coriander. Serve immediately, garnished with lime wedges.

# Crispy chilli orange grilled chicken

Nutrition notes per serving:
★ calories 448
★ protein 34 g
★ carbohydrate 12 g
★ fat 30 g
★ saturated fat 0.8 g
★ fibre 1 g
★ added sugar 8 g
★ salt 0.65 g

When it comes to chicken I'm a thigh man as I think they have the best flavour and are also the most succulent – by all means use breast, just cook for about 10 minutes longer. Try this with a good spoonful of my Chilli Ginger Jam (page 142).

Preparation time: 5 minutes • Cooking time: 20 minutes • Serves 4

2 tablespoons olive oil
2 garlic cloves, thinly sliced
2 tablespoons light muscovado sugar
1–2 teaspoons dried chilli flakes
8 large boneless, skin-on chicken thighs

1 large orange, cut into wedges
salt and freshly ground black pepper
grated rind of 1 lime, to garnish
lightly dressed leafy salad or steamed
  fragrant rice, to serve

**1** Combine the oil in a large bowl with the garlic, sugar and chilli flakes – the amount you use depends on how hot you like your food. Slash the skin of each chicken thigh to help the flavours to penetrate, and then add to the bowl with half the orange wedges. Season generously and mix until well combined. Cover with clingfilm and set aside for at least 15 minutes to allow the flavours to develop (or up to 2 hours in the fridge is fine if time allows).

**2** Heat a griddle or a heavy-based frying-pan until smoking hot. Place the chicken pieces skin-side down on to the hot pan and leave to cook for 4 minutes without moving, then carefully turn over; if the chicken is sticking, this means that it is not ready to be turned, so leave it for a minute or so longer.

**3** Once all the chicken has been turned, reduce the heat slightly and continue to cook for another 6–7 minutes or until the skin is crisp and the chicken is tender and cooked through. Place the chicken on to serving plates and quickly grill the reserved orange wedges: this will only take a minute or so in a hot pan and the bar marks look great. Place around the chicken, top with the lime rind and serve with leafy salad or steamed rice, and my Chilli Ginger Jam.

Boneless chicken thighs are available from some supermarkets, or just ask your butcher to bone them for you.

# Flambé tequila chicken with pine nuts

Nutrition notes per serving:
★ calories 428
★ protein 38 g
★ carbohydrate 8 g
★ fat 24 g
★ saturated fat 4 g
★ fibre 2 g
★ added sugar 1 g
★ salt 1.11 g

For those evenings when you want the food to reflect the mood and yet want to be involved in the party instead of being stuck in the kitchen, this boozy little number could be right up your street.

Preparation time: 5 minutes • Cooking time: 20 minutes • Serves 4

3 tablespoons pine nuts
4 tablespoons sunflower oil
8 boneless, skinless chicken thighs
1 onion, sliced
2 garlic cloves, finely chopped
4 tablespoons tequila
1 tablespoon tomato purée
a 400 g (14 oz) can chopped tomatoes

a dash of Tabasco
1 teaspoon paprika
1 teaspoon sugar
300 ml (½ pint) chicken stock
salt and freshly ground black pepper
snipped fresh chives, to garnish
steamed basmati rice, to serve

1 Heat a small frying-pan and toast the pine nuts for 2–3 minutes until golden, remove from the pan and set aside.

2 Heat 2 tablespoons of oil in a large, heavy-based pan with a lid. Add the chicken and cook over a moderate heat for about 6 minutes, turning once. Remove from the pan and set aside.

3 Add the remaining oil to the pan and gently fry the onion and garlic for 3–4 minutes until softened but not coloured, stirring occasionally. Add 2 tablespoons of the tequila and carefully flambé (see tip). Stir in the tomato purée, chopped tomatoes, Tabasco, paprika and sugar and cook for a few minutes.

4 Pour in the stock and return the chicken to the pan, then cover and simmer for another 10 minutes until the chicken is tender and the sauce has slightly reduced. Pour in the remaining 2 tablespoons of tequila and heat through for 2 minutes. Season to taste. Scatter over the pine nuts and a sprinkling of chives, and serve with basmati rice.

To flambé safely, toss the ingredients to the front of the pan, tilt the pan away from you and pour in the tequila. Light the tequila, shake the pan and leave until the flames go out.

# Tempting turkey, leek and mushroom pies

Nutrition notes per serving:
* calories 596
* protein 37 g
* carbohydrate 25 g
* fat 37 g
* saturated fat 15 g
* fibre 2 g
* added sugar none
* salt 0.87 g

These pies are fab served with my garlic mash (page 101). You could also substitute the turkey with chicken, and, if you like a bit of kick to your food, try adding 1 teaspoon of cayenne pepper to the flour.

Preparation time: 15 minutes • Cooking time: 40 minutes • Serves 4

2 tablespoons plain flour, plus a little extra for dusting

500 g (1lb 2 oz) turkey breast steaks, trimmed and cut into bite-sized pieces

4 tablespoons olive oil

2 leeks, trimmed and sliced (white part only)

150 g (5 oz) chestnut mushrooms, sliced

2 garlic cloves, crushed

120 ml (4 fl oz) dry white wine

150 ml (¼ pint ) chicken stock (see tip)

120 ml (4 fl oz) double cream

2–3 tablespoons chopped fresh flat-leaf parsley

150 g (5 oz) ready-rolled puff pastry, thawed if frozen

1 egg yolk mixed with 1 tablespoon of water

salt and freshly ground black pepper

1 Pre-heat the oven to 220°C/425°F/Gas 7/fan oven 200°C. Place the flour in a large bowl and season generously, then use to coat the turkey pieces, shaking off any excess. Heat 2 table-spoons of oil in a large, heavy-based pan, add the turkey pieces and cook for a minute or two on each side until beginning to brown. Remove from the pan and set aside.

2 Add the remaining oil to the pan, then stir in the leeks, mushrooms and garlic and cook over a medium heat for 3 minutes until softened but not coloured. Return the turkey to the pan, then pour in the wine, bring to the boil and cook for another 1–2 minutes, scraping the bottom of the pan with a wooden spoon to remove any sediment.

3 Pour the stock into the pan with the cream and simmer for 6 minutes until slightly reduced and thickened, stirring occasionally, then stir in the parsley and season to taste. Ladle the mixture into 4 x 300 ml (½ pint) individual pie dishes; allow to cool slightly so that a light skin forms on top.

4 Meanwhile, roll out the pastry to about 5 mm (¼ inch) thick on a lightly floured work surface and cut out 4 lids large enough to fit the top of your pies. Brush the lips of the pie dishes with the egg wash and stick down the pastry lids. Egg wash the top of each lid and gently press down along the sides to seal. Cut a small slit in each pie lid. Brush with the egg wash and bake for about 25 minutes or until the pies are golden brown. Serve immediately.

If you can't buy fresh chicken stock, use half a chicken stock cube dissolved in 150 ml (¼ pint) boiling water.

# Meaty
# ma

# ins

Stir-fried ginger pork with squeaky greens • Lamb tagine with minted, herbed couscous • Pan-roasted pork with white bean purée • Beef wellington parcels with red-wine jus • Sirloin skewers with sweet peppers and shiitake • Szechuan peppered steak with spiced redcurrants • Harissa-glazed lamb with saffron rice • Venison steaks with stewed plums and garlic mash • Sausage and pea risotto • Wrapped pancetta lamb burgers

# Stir-fried ginger pork with squeaky greens

Nutrition notes per serving:
★ calories 294
★ protein 24 g
★ carbohydrate 7 g
★ fat 18 g
★ saturated fat 3 g
★ fibre 2 g
★ added sugar 1 g
★ salt 2.38 g

This has to be one of my favourite ways of preparing greens. The stir-frying keeps their crunch while the hot sauce gives them a rich, almost nutty flavour.

Preparation time: 20 minutes • Cooking time: 20 minutes • Serves 4

450 g (1 lb) boneless pork loin chops
2 tablespoons dry sherry or rice wine
2 tablespoons dark soy sauce
1 tablespoon sesame oil
2 teaspoons cornflour
120 ml (4 fl oz) chicken stock
3 tablespoons sunflower oil
a 5 cm (2 inch) piece fresh root ginger, finely grated

2 salad onions, cut into 2 cm (¾ inch) pieces
2 tablespoons sweet chilli sauce
275 g (10 oz) mixed prepared green vegetables (see tip)
salt and freshly ground black pepper
red chilli rings and shredded spring onion, to garnish
Thai fragrant rice, to serve

1 Trim any excess fat from the side of each pork chop, then thinly slice the meat against the grain. Put half of the sherry or rice wine and soy sauce in a shallow, non-metallic dish and add the sesame oil and cornflour, and season to taste. Stir in the pork and set aside for 15 minutes (up to 24 hours covered with clingfilm in the fridge is fine).

2 Put the chicken stock in a small pan over a low heat. Heat a wok until hot, add 2 tablespoons of the sunflower oil and swirl around, tip in the pork and stir-fry for 3–4 minutes until well sealed and lightly golden. Transfer to a plate.

3 Add another tablespoon of oil to the wok and stir-fry the ginger and salad onions for 20 seconds, then add the chilli sauce and cook for another minute until aromatic. Tip in the green vegetables and continue to stir-fry for 2–3 minutes until they are heated through and any leaves are just beginning to wilt.

4 Return the pork to the wok, stir in the hot stock and remaining sherry or wine and soy and, once it starts to bubble, reduce the heat and season to taste. Serve on top of steamed Thai fragrant rice with a few chilli rings and some shredded spring onion sprinkled over, to garnish.

There's a whole range of green vegetables that you could use for this dish – try sugar-snap peas, French beans, mangetout, Swiss chard or pak choi.

# Lamb tagine with minted, herbed couscous

Nutrition notes per serving:
- calories 604
- protein 41 g
- carbohydrate 36 g
- fat 33 g
- saturated fat 10 g
- fibre 2 g
- added sugar 3 g
- salt 1.29 g

This gorgeous tagine may seem like it's got a lot of ingredients, but I promise the results are worth it. Get your butcher to prepare the lamb for you – it's their job and can save you a good deal of time.

Preparation time: 15 minutes • Cooking time: 40 minutes • Serves 4–6

1 tablespoon paprika
1 teaspoon each ground coriander, turmeric, cinnamon and cumin
750 g (1½ lb) lamb leg steaks, well trimmed and cut into bite-sized chunks
6 tablespoons extra-virgin olive oil
1 large onion, roughly chopped
2 garlic cloves, chopped
a 2.5 cm (1 inch) piece peeled fresh root ginger, chopped

1.2 litres (2 pints) chicken stock
a 400 g (14 oz) can chopped tomatoes
1 tablespoon clear honey
175 g (6 oz) couscous
juice of 1 lemon
2 tablespoons chopped fresh, mixed flat-leaf parsley and mint
salt and cracked black pepper
thick Greek yoghurt and fresh coriander leaves, to garnish

1 Heat a large, heavy-based pan. Mix together the spices and 1 teaspoon of pepper in a large bowl. Add the lamb and, using your hands, rub in the spice mixture. Add 1 tablespoon of the olive oil to the heated pan and quickly brown half the spiced lamb. Transfer to a plate and repeat with another tablespoon of oil and the remaining lamb.

2 Meanwhile, place the onion, garlic and ginger in a food processor or mini blender and pulse until finely minced. Add another tablespoon of oil to the pan, then add the onion mixture and sauté for 3–4 minutes until softened and coloured from the spices left in the bottom of the pan. Return the lamb to the pan.

3 Pour in half of the stock, and all of the tomatoes and honey, stirring to combine. Bring to the boil, season with salt, then reduce the heat and simmer for about 30 minutes until the lamb is tender and the sauce has thickened and reduced. Season to taste.

4 Meanwhile, make the couscous. Place it in a bowl and add 2 tablespoons of the oil and the lemon juice, stirring to ensure all the grains are completely coated. Heat the remaining stock in a small pan and season generously. Pour the seasoned stock over the couscous and set aside for about 10 minutes until all the liquid has been absorbed, then stir in the remaining tablespoon of olive oil and the herbs. Serve the couscous and lamb tagine in warmed bowls with a dollop of Greek yoghurt and a few sprigs of coriander.

# Pan-roasted pork with white bean purée

Nutrition notes per serving:
- calories 1148
- protein 72 g
- carbohydrate 44 g
- fat 77 g
- saturated fat 31 g
- fibre 13 g
- added sugar 2 g
- salt 2.02 g

For a healthy alternative to a creamy mash I always turn to white bean purée, which is especially moreish flavoured with Wensleydale cheese, although Cheddar would be a good alternative if you can't get hold of Wensleydale.

Preparation time: 25 minutes • Cooking time: 20 minutes • Serves 2

5 tablespoons extra-virgin olive oil
2 teaspoons each finely chopped, fresh rosemary and thyme
a 400 g (14 oz) piece pork fillet, trimmed
1 apple, peeled, halved and cored
50 g (2 oz) unsalted butter
½ teaspoon light muscovado sugar
1 onion, finely chopped
2 garlic cloves, crushed

400 g (14 oz) can cannellini beans, drained and rinsed
100 g (4 oz) Wensleydale, crumbled
1 tablespoon each chopped fresh flat-leaf parsley and chives
about 4–5 tablespoons chicken stock
a good pinch of caraway seeds
½ Savoy cabbage, cored and shredded
salt and freshly ground black pepper

1 Pre-heat the oven to 200°C/400°F/Gas 6/fan oven 180°C. Place 1 tablespoon of olive oil, the rosemary and thyme into a shallow dish, and season generously with black pepper. Add the pork, and turn to coat evenly.

2 Heat an ovenproof frying-pan until hot. Add the pork and cook for 1–2 minutes on each side until a little brown and well sealed. Add the apple halves to the pan with a knob of the butter, then turn them cut-side up and sprinkle over the sugar. Transfer to the oven and roast for 10–12 minutes or until the pork is tender and the apples have caramelized. Remove from the oven and rest in a warm place for about 10 minutes.

3 Meanwhile, place 2 tablespoons of olive oil and half the butter in a heavy-based pan. Add the onion and garlic and sauté for about 5 minutes until softened but not coloured. Stir in the beans and cook for another few minutes until heated through. Mix in the cheese and, when melted, blitz with a hand blender to a rough purée. Stir in the herbs, then season and add 1–2 tablespoons of the stock, if necessary.

4 To sauté the cabbage, heat a wok or frying-pan and add the remaining olive oil and butter. Tip in the caraway seeds and cabbage and sauté for 1–2 minutes until softened. Add the remaining stock, season and cook for a few minutes until most of the liquid has evaporated. Carve the pork on the diagonal. Divide the bean purée between warmed serving plates and add a mound of cabbage. Arrange the pork on top and add an apple half to serve.

Savoy cabbage provides some extra colour and texture to this dish, but you could always use another variety of cabbage, such as York or January King, depending on what's available.

# Beef wellington parcels with red-wine jus

Nutrition notes per serving:
★ calories 768
★ protein 48 g
★ carbohydrate 29 g
★ fat 49 g
★ saturated fat 18 g
★ fibre 1 g
★ added sugar none
★ salt 1.24 g

An all-time classic dish. Perhaps it's the wonderful textures – juicy fillet steak, concentrated wild mushrooms and pâté in a very crisp pastry crust. The parcels are brilliant for entertaining as they can be made several hours in advance.

Preparation time: 20 minutes • Cooking time: 40 minutes • Serves 4

50 g (2 oz) unsalted butter, diced and chilled, plus extra for greasing
2 tablespoons olive oil, for frying
1 large onion, finely chopped
2 garlic cloves, crushed
225 g (8 oz) flat mushrooms, chopped
10 g (⅓ oz) dried porcini mushrooms soaked in boiling water for 20 minutes, then drained and finely chopped
1 tablespoon chopped fresh flat-leaf parsley

4 x 175 g (6 oz) fillet steaks, each about 2.5 cm (1 inch) thick
100 g (4 oz) smooth chicken liver pâté
250 g (9 oz) ready-made puff pastry, thawed if frozen
plain flour, for dusting
1 large egg, beaten
175 ml (6 fl oz) red wine
salt and freshly ground black pepper
broccoli, to serve

1 Pre-heat the oven to 220°C/425°F/Gas 7/fan oven 200°C. To make the filling, melt half the butter with half the oil in a frying-pan. Add the onion, garlic, and all the mushrooms and sauté for 10 minutes until tender and all the liquid has evaporated. Stir in the parsley, tip into a bowl, season and cool.

2 Season the steaks. Wipe out the same frying-pan and heat until hot. Add the remaining oil and sear the seasoned steaks for 20–30 seconds on all sides. Cool, then spread over the pâté. Cut the pastry into 4 pieces, roll out on a lightly floured surface to 20 cm (8 inch) squares and brush with beaten egg. Divide the mushroom mixture between the squares and place a steak on top, pâté-side down. Bring up two opposite corners of the pastry square to overlap the steak in the centre, seal and gently tuck in the sides, brush with a little beaten egg, and bring the remaining two corners up and seal. Place the parcels on a heated non-stick baking sheet, brush with beaten egg and bake in the oven for 25 minutes for medium-rare, or 5 minutes more for well done.

3 Place the frying-pan that you used to cook the steaks back on the heat. Pour in the wine and allow to bubble down, then simmer until reduced by two-thirds. Just before serving, whisk in the remaining 25 g (1 oz) of the butter and season. Serve the beef wellingtons on warmed plates with the broccoli, and a little of the red-wine jus spooned over.

Dried porcini mushrooms are readily available in 10 g (⅓ oz) packets and have the most intense mushroom flavour.

# **low fat!** Sirloin skewers with sweet peppers and shiitake

Nutrition notes per serving:
- calories 382
- protein 38 g
- carbohydrate 29 g
- fat 11 g
- saturated fat 3 g
- fibre 2 g
- added sugar 0.5 g
- salt 3.23 g

This dish is full of fresh, clean flavours and the sauce created is similar to teriyaki but not quite as sweet. Shiitake mushrooms are excellent in all manner of Oriental dishes as they have a pronounced mushroomy scent and flavour.

Preparation time: 20 minutes • Cooking time: 15 minutes • Serves 4

2 teaspoons sesame oil
4 tablespoons dark soy sauce
6 tablespoons sake or dry white wine
1 tablespoon freshly grated root ginger
2 garlic cloves, finely chopped
550 g (1¼ lb) sirloin steak, cut into
  2.5 cm (1 inch) cubes
1 tablespoon sunflower oil

2 large red peppers, seeded and cut into
  4 cm (1½ inch) slices
a 120 g (4½ oz) packet shiitake
  mushrooms, trimmed and halved
1 bunch salad onions, trimmed and cut
  into 4 cm (1½ inch) lengths
salt and freshly ground black pepper
fragrant jasmine rice, to serve

1 Place the sesame oil, soy sauce, sake or wine, ginger and garlic in a shallow, non-metallic dish. Season to taste and stir in the steak cubes, stirring to combine, then set aside to marinate for 10 minutes at room temperature (or cover with clingfilm and chill for up to 24 hours).

2 Heat a large, non-stick frying-pan. Drain the steak from the marinade, reserving it to use later, then thread the steak on to 8 x 15 cm (6 inch) wooden skewers. When the pan is smoking hot, add the skewers and sear on all sides – you may have to do this in two batches, depending on the size of your pan. Transfer to a warmed plate and keep warm.

3 Add the sunflower oil to the same pan, and then tip in the peppers and mushrooms. Sauté for 2 minutes, then add the salad onions and sauté for another minute. Add the reserved marinade, reduce the heat and continue to cook for about 1 minute or until the vegetables are just tender and the sauce has slightly thickened, stirring occasionally. Check the seasoning then arrange the vegetables on warmed serving plates with the skewers on top and spoon over any remaining sauce. Serve with fragrant jasmine rice.

When preparing mushrooms, don't be tempted to wash or peel them. Just wipe away any dirt with a damp cloth.

# Szechuan peppered steak
# with spiced redcurrants

The best way to remove redcurrants from their stems is to use a fork; hold the end of the stem and push through the prongs, dragging the fork downwards. Not only does it save time but it also doesn't damage the delicate fruit.

Preparation time: 10 minutes • Cooking time: 15–20 minutes • Serves 4

1 tablespoon Szechuan peppercorns
1 tablespoon black peppercorns
4 x 150 g (5 oz) rump steaks, well trimmed
1 tablespoon sunflower oil
75 g (3 oz) sugar
a pinch of dried chilli flakes

1 cinnamon stick, crushed into tiny pieces, or 1 teaspoon ground cinnamon
200 g (7 oz) redcurrants, removed from stalks (see introduction)
50 g (2 oz) unsalted butter
salt
sautéed new potatoes, to serve (optional)

1 Using a pestle and mortar, grind the peppercorns – you don't need a fine powder, a bit of texture is good. Rub each of the steaks with a little oil to help the peppercorns to stick, and then press the peppercorn mixture on to each steak, making sure they are evenly coated. Arrange on a large plate, cover loosely with clingfilm, then set aside at room temperature.

2 Meanwhile, place the sugar in a small, heavy-based pan with 2 tablespoons of water. Cook over a gentle heat for a couple of minutes, stirring until the sugar has completely dissolved. Increase the heat, bring to the boil and add the chilli and cinnamon, then boil fast for 1 minute. Add the redcurrants, bring to a gentle simmer and cook for 4–5 minutes or until the currants are starting to soften but are still holding their shape. Remove from the heat and allow to stand for a few minutes so that the flavours can combine.

3 Melt the butter in a large, non-stick frying-pan. When the butter is starting to foam, add the steaks and cook for 2 minutes, then turn, reduce the heat slightly and cook for another 3 minutes for rare. If you prefer your steaks medium, increase the cooking time by 1 minute for each side; or for well done, increase by 2 minutes for each side. Transfer the steaks to warmed serving plates and season with salt to taste. Leave to rest for a few minutes, then add a good dollop of the spiced redcurrants to each plate with some sautéed potatoes, if liked. Serve immediately.

Szechuan peppercorns are more aromatic than pepper-corns. They are not related to peppercorns, but are the dried berries of an oriental shrub called the prickly ash tree.

# Harissa-glazed lamb with saffron rice

Nutrition notes per serving:
- calories 654
- protein 34 g
- carbohydrate 44 g
- fat 39 g
- saturated fat 18 g
- fibre 0.1 g
- added sugar 3 g
- salt 0.6 g

This is a delightful dish with a truly evocative North African taste. Harissa is widely available in the special selection or gourmet foods section of supermarkets or in good delis. Once opened, it will keep in your fridge for a few weeks.

Preparation time: 10 minutes • Cooking time: 15–20 minutes • Serves 4

4 x 150–175 g (5–6 oz) lamb leg steaks, about 2.5 cm (1 inch) thick
2 tablespoons harissa paste (see introduction)
1 tablespoon tomato purée
1 tablespoon clear honey

2 tablespoons olive oil
a pinch of saffron strands
75 g (3 oz) unsalted butter
200 g (7 oz) basmati rice, well rinsed
4 cardamom pods, cracked
salt and freshly ground black pepper

1 Season the lamb steaks with pepper and place in a shallow, non-metallic dish. Mix the harissa, tomato purée, honey and oil in a small bowl and rub all over the lamb. Cover with clingfilm and set aside for 5 minutes to marinate (or overnight in the fridge is best, if time allows).

2 Place the saffron strands in a small bowl and pour over 3 tablespoons of boiling water. Set aside to infuse for about 5 minutes. Melt the butter in a large, heavy-based pan with a lid. When it starts to foam, tip in the rice and cardamom pods, then stir over a medium heat for 2 minutes until all the rice grains are well coated with the butter. Add a teaspoon of salt then pour in enough boiling water to cover the rice by 2.5 cm (1 inch) and bring to a simmer, then cover and cook for 5 minutes. Remove the lid and stir in the saffron mixture. Cover again and continue to cook for another 5 minutes until the rice is just tender but retains some bite.

3 Meanwhile, heat a griddle-pan. Add the marinated lamb steaks and cook for 5–7 minutes, turning once or twice. If you like your meat more well done, then increase the cooking time by 3 minutes. When cooked, allow the lamb to rest for a couple of minutes so it becomes nice and tender. Serve whole or carve into slices on a slant and arrange on top of the saffron rice.

Use any left-over harissa paste to jazz up a piece of meat or even firm-fleshed fish, such as salmon, tuna or swordfish. Just make sure you use it in moderation as it has quite a kick!

# Venison steaks with stewed plums and garlic mash

Nutrition notes per serving:
calories 632
protein 40 g
carbohydrate 61 g
fat 24 g
saturated fat 8 g
fibre 5 g
added sugar 10 g
salt 0.52 g

I love venison and believe it is vastly underrated. I have used fillet steaks in this recipe, which are not cut from the same place as a beef fillet, but are actually cut from the sirloin. They are far superior to any other cut of venison.

Preparation time: 10 minutes • Cooking time: 15 minutes • Serves 4

8 garlic cloves, unpeeled
4 tablespoons olive oil
900 g (2 lb) potatoes, peeled and cut
  into cubes
85 ml (3 fl oz) ruby red port or red wine
2 tablespoons sugar

8 large plums, stones removed and flesh
  quartered
4 x 150 g (5 oz) venison fillet steaks
50 g (2 oz) unsalted butter
about 2 tablespoons milk
salt and freshly ground black pepper

1  Place the garlic and 2 tablespoons of the oil in a small frying-pan and cook over a low heat for 8–10 minutes until the garlic cloves are completely tender but not coloured. Remove from the heat and set aside to cool. Place the potatoes in a large pan of boiling salted water, cover and simmer for 10–12 minutes or until completely tender.

2  Meanwhile, pour the port or red wine into a pan and add the sugar. Heat gently for a couple of minutes until the sugar has dissolved, stirring occasionally. Tip in the plums, bring to a simmer and cook for 5–8 minutes or until the plums are softened but still holding their shape – this will depend on their ripeness.

3  Heat a large, heavy-based frying-pan until very hot. Rub the remaining 2 tablespoons of oil all over the venison steaks and season to taste. Add to the heated pan and cook for 2 minutes, then turn over and cook for another 3 minutes for rare. If you prefer your meat medium increase cooking time by 1 minute on each side; or for well done increase by 2 minutes on each side. Remove from the heat and set aside in a warm place to rest.

4  Drain the potatoes, and mash until smooth, then beat in the butter and add enough milk to make a smooth purée. Squeeze the pulp from the cooled garlic cloves into the mash and then beat until evenly combined. Season to taste.

5  Carve the venison steaks and arrange on warmed serving plates on a pile of the roasted garlic mash. Spoon a few of the stewed plum quarters to one side and serve immediately.

# Sausage and pea risotto

Nutrition notes per serving:
- calories 745
- protein 30 g
- carbohydrate 80 g
- fat 36 g
- saturated fat 17 g
- fibre 4 g
- added sugar none
- salt 3.66 g

My kids go crazy for this dish. You can change the flavour completely by using one of the variety of high-quality sausages that are now widely available from supermarkets and good butchers, such as pork and leek, or Toulouse.

Preparation time: 5 minutes • Cooking time: 30 minutes • Serves 4

450 g (1 lb) good-quality butcher's pork
  sausages, about 6 in total
50 g (2 oz) unsalted butter
1 small onion, finely chopped
2 garlic cloves, crushed
350 g (12 oz) Arborio (risotto) rice
1.2 litres (2 pints) chicken stock

150 g (5 oz) frozen peas or petit pois
6 tablespoons freshly grated Parmesan,
  plus extra to garnish
2 tablespoons roughly chopped fresh
  flat-leaf parsley
salt and freshly ground black pepper

1 Pre-heat the grill to medium. Arrange the sausages on a grill rack and grill for 10–15 minutes, depending on the thickness, turning every 2–3 minutes until cooked through and golden brown. Transfer to a plate and leave until cool enough to handle, then cut into chunky slices and set aside.

2 Melt the butter in a large, shallow pan. Add the onion and garlic and cook gently for about 4–5 minutes until softened but not coloured, stirring occasionally. Increase the heat, stir in the rice and cook gently for 1 minute, stirring continuously, until the rice is opaque.

3 Meanwhile, pour the stock into a separate pan and bring to a gentle simmer. Add a ladleful of stock to the rice mixture and allow to reduce, stirring until it is completely absorbed. Continue to add the simmering stock a ladleful at a time, stirring frequently. Allow each stock addition to be almost completely absorbed before adding the next ladleful.

4 After about 20 minutes, when the rice is nearly cooked, tip the peas into the remaining stock and simmer for 2 minutes before adding to the risotto. When the risotto is ready it should be just tender but still have a little bite. Season to taste, then stir in the Parmesan and parsley until combined, then fold in the sausages. Season to taste and divide among warmed serving bowls or plates. Garnish with some Parmesan and serve immediately.

If you're cooking for adults, stir in a glass of wine before adding the stock, and a few tablespoons of double cream at the finish. It'll taste even more delicious, I guarantee.

# Wrapped pancetta lamb burgers

An ideal way to serve these lamb burgers would be in a pitta pocket, as described below. Otherwise, make the burgers larger and serve them with rice and vegetables – just remember to double the cooking time.

Preparation time: 15 minutes • Cooking time: 10 minutes • Serves 4

4 tablespoons finely chopped onion
2 garlic cloves, crushed
2 tablespoons double cream
1 teaspoon fresh thyme leaves
2 teaspoons paprika (preferably smoked)
375 g (13 oz) lean minced lamb
8 thin slices pancetta
2 tablespoons olive oil
salt and freshly ground black pepper

warmed small pitta pockets, salad leaves, sliced tomatoes, raw onion rings, to serve
*For the minted yoghurt dip*
200 ml (7 fl oz) thick Greek yoghurt
¼ cucumber, grated and with the water squeezed out (see tip)
a handful of fresh mint leaves, shredded
1 garlic clove, crushed

1 To make the minted yoghurt dip, combine the Greek yoghurt, cucumber, mint leaves and garlic in a small bowl. Season to taste, spoon into a clean bowl and set aside.

2 In a food processor, briefly blitz the onion, garlic, cream, thyme and paprika. Add the minced lamb, season generously and continue to blitz in short bursts until just combined. You could also do this by hand in a bowl. Divide the mixture into 8 then, with slightly wet hands, roll into balls and flatten slightly to make patties that are about 5 cm (2 inches) wide. Carefully wrap a slice of pancetta around each patty in a criss-cross style.

3 Heat the oil in a large frying-pan and cook the burgers over a medium heat for about 3–4 minutes on each side, until slightly browned but still a little pink in the centre. Cut the burgers in half.

4 Split the pitta pockets and fill each half with the salad leaves, tomato slices, onions and two burger halves. Drizzle over a little of the minted yoghurt dip and serve at once.

To squeeze the water out of a cucumber, place the grated flesh in a clean tea towel and squeeze gently until any excess water has been forced out.

# Fresh and fabu
## veg

# lous
# etarian

Potato-pastry tart with leeks and mushrooms • Penne pecorino and broad bean gratin • Easy fragrant rice with peas • Layered summer picnic potato salads • Chickpea and spinach curry with flat bread • Courgette, coriander and parmesan röstis • Squash and pine nut risotto with rocket pesto • Huevos rancheros • Baked tomatoes with puy lentils and goats' cheese • Tagliatelle with roasted walnut and herb pesto

# Potato-pastry tart with leeks and mushrooms

Nutrition notes per serving:
calories 441
protein 8 g
carbohydrate 28 g
fat 34 g
saturated fat 18 g
fibre 3 g
added sugar none
salt 0.79 g

Potato pastry is great for using up a small bowl of mashed potato and can be used instead of shortcrust pastry for any savoury tart or quiche. Just be careful not to over-handle it or it will become tough.

Preparation time: 20 minutes • Cooking time: 45 minutes • Serves 4

100 g (4 oz) plain flour, plus extra for dusting
75 g (3 oz) unsalted butter, diced and chilled
100 g (4 oz) smooth mashed potato
about 1 tablespoon iced water (optional)
2 tablespoons olive oil
400 g (14 oz) leeks, well trimmed and thinly sliced

100 g (4 oz) chestnut mushrooms, sliced
75 g (3 oz) mascarpone cheese
50 g (2 oz) Gorgonzola, dolcelatte or Roquefort, diced
a pinch of crushed dried chillies (optional)
salt and freshly ground black pepper
lightly dressed fresh green salad, to serve (optional)

1 Pre-heat the oven to 200°C/400°F/Gas Mark 6/fan oven 180°C. To make the potato pastry, sift the flour into a bowl with plenty of seasoning. Rub in the butter until the mixture resembles fine breadcrumbs. Quickly mix in the mashed potato and, if necessary, add a little iced water until you have achieved a soft dough. Knead lightly into a ball and then wrap in clingfilm and chill for at least 10 minutes to rest.

2 Heat the oil in a frying-pan, add the leeks and fry gently for about 5 minutes until softened but not coloured, stirring occasionally. Add the mushrooms and cook for another few minutes until just tender. Season well, remove from the heat and leave to cool.

3 Gently roll out the pastry to a 25 cm (10 inch) round on a lightly floured surface. Transfer to a baking sheet lined with non-stick baking paper and pinch the edges to make a rim. Stir the mascarpone into the leek mixture, and then spoon over the pastry. Scatter the blue cheese on top of the tart with a sprinkling of crushed chillies, if using. Bake for 25–30 minutes or until the pastry rim is golden brown. Serve cut into slices with salad, if liked.

## VARIATIONS

**Artichoke and Mushroom:** substitute a drained jar of wood-roasted artichoke hearts for the leeks and simply slice them and mix with the cooked mushrooms before using.

**Tomato and Mozzarella:** spread the potato pastry with a tablespoon of pesto and then cover with overlapping slices of tomatoes and mozzarella. Drizzle over a little basil or chilli oil and season with cracked black pepper.

**Smoky Bacon and Leek:** gently fry strips of smoked streaky bacon or pancetta until the fat runs and use instead of the mushrooms for a non-vegetarian alternative; or try using scraps of hand-carved cooked ham.

# Penne pecorino and broad bean gratin

Nutrition notes per serving:
calories 1235
protein 36 g
carbohydrate 86 g
fat 80 g
saturated fat 47 g
fibre 14 g
added sugar none
salt 1.22 g

The broad beans add a wonderful texture to this pasta gratin, while the flavoured mascarpone cream helps keep everything moist. Broad beans take a bit of time to slip out of their skins but the end result is stunning.

Preparation time: 20 minutes • Cooking time: 25 minutes • Serves 4

350 g (12 oz) good quality penne pasta
300 ml (½ pint) dry white wine
300 ml (½ pint) double cream
750 g (1¾ lb) fresh or frozen broad beans
250 g (9 oz) mascarpone cheese
2 egg yolks

2 tablespoons snipped fresh chives
2 tablespoons shredded fresh basil
25 g (1 oz) freshly grated Parmesan
75 g (3 oz) freshly grated pecorino
salt and freshly ground pepper
lightly dressed Italian salad leaves, to serve (optional)

1 Plunge the penne in a large pan of boiling salted water and cook for 8–10 minutes or according to the packet instructions until al dente. Drain and refresh under cold running water. Reduce the white wine in a small pan until it has evaporated to about 2 tablespoons. Add the cream and bring to the boil, then season and lower the heat. Simmer gently for 6–8 minutes until slightly reduced and thickened. Leave to cool slightly.

2 Place the broad beans in a pan of boiling salted water and cook for 2–3 minutes or until just tender. Drain and refresh under cold running water, then slip the beans out of their skins. Fold the broad beans into the cooked penne and tip into a shallow ovenproof dish.

3 Pre-heat the grill to medium. Beat together the mascarpone cheese, egg yolks, chives and basil in a bowl with the Parmesan and most of the pecorino, reserving a handful to sprinkle on top. Spoon over the broad beans and penne until completely covered, then scatter over the reserved pecorino. Place under the grill and cook for 5–10 minutes until heated through, bubbling and lightly golden. Serve straight from the dish at the table with a dressed Italian salad, if liked.

# Easy fragrant rice
## with peas

Nutrition notes per serving:
calories 1010
protein 26 g
carbohydrate 175 g
fat 27 g
saturated fat 4 g
fibre 14 g
added sugar none
salt 1.2 g

Whenever I cook rice I cook extra so that I can use it in this dish because it's so sensational. To prevent left-over rice going lumpy, stir in a splash of oil before refrigerating it. I've also included lots of variations (see opposite) to inspire you.

Preparation time: 10 minutes • Cooking time: 20 minutes • Serves 2

2 tablespoons sunflower oil
2 onions, halved and cut lengthways
   into slivers
2 garlic cloves, finely chopped
1 tablespoon freshly grated root ginger
100 g (4 oz) mushrooms, sliced

1 teaspoon ground turmeric
1–2 teaspoons hot chilli powder
450 g (1 lb) cooked rice (see
   introduction)
175 g (6 oz) frozen peas
salt and freshly ground black pepper

1 Heat a wok or large frying-pan until hot. Add the oil and then tip in the onions and stir-fry for 4–5 minutes until they are sizzling and just starting to brown.

2 Add the garlic to the wok with the ginger and mushrooms, season and continue to stir-fry for another 2–3 minutes until the mushrooms are just tender. Add the turmeric and enough chilli powder to taste (depending on how hot you like your food), stirring well to combine.

3 Add the rice to the onion mixture with the peas and continue to stir-fry for another 2–3 minutes or until the rice is thoroughly hot and has picked up plenty of colour and the peas are tender. Season to taste and serve at once.

## VARIATIONS

**Baby spinach leaves**: added just after the spices but before the rice, with a handful of toasted pine nuts, if liked.

**Egg strips**: 2 eggs whisked with a dash of soy and swirled up the sides of a heated wok with a tablespoon of oil in it. This then gets rolled up like a pancake and shredded before adding to the rice to just warm through.

**Broccoli**: blanched florets added instead of the peas. Just before serving, finish with a mixture of sliced red chillies and salad onions that have been stir-fried in a little oil and seasoned.

### ... and for some non-vegetarian options

**Chorizo**: chopped or sliced and added to the pan with the onions – this not only gives the rice a wonderful flavour but adds great colour to the dish.

**Sunday's roast**: the meat stripped from the bones and cut into bite-sized pieces before adding at the same stage as the rice with any leftover gravy or pan juices.

**Cooked diced chicken**: stir-fried for a minute in a little oil and folded in just before serving.

# Layered summer picnic potato salads

Nutrition notes per serving:
- calories 403
- protein 11 g
- carbohydrate 25 g
- fat 29 g
- saturated fat 5 g
- fibre 4 g
- added sugar 1 g
- salt 0.7 g

These individual salads need nothing more than a hunk of bread to turn them into a feast fit for a king. They will also transport brilliantly in the bowls for a picnic, ready to be turned out when you get to your destination.

Preparation time: 20 minutes • Cooking time: 15 minutes • Serves 4

450 g (1 lb) small new potatoes, scrubbed
225 g (8 oz) French beans, trimmed and cut in half
4 eggs (preferably organic or free-range)
1 tablespoon white wine vinegar
2 teaspoons Dijon mustard
1 teaspoon sugar

8 tablespoons extra-virgin olive oil
1 tablespoon snipped fresh chives
450 g (1 lb) cherry tomatoes, halved
50 g (2 oz) crisp green lettuce (such as cos or romaine), shredded
salt and freshly ground black pepper
crusty bread, to serve

1 Slice the potatoes into fairly thick discs and place in a pan of boiling salted water, cover and cook for 10–15 minutes until tender. Just before the end of cooking time, steam the beans in a colander on top of the boiling potatoes for 2–3 minutes, and refresh under cold water.

2 Boil the eggs for 7–8 minutes (3–4 minutes longer if you like them really hard-boiled). Drain, run under cold running water, peel off the shells and cut each one into quarters.

3 Place the vinegar, mustard, sugar and some seasoning in a screw-topped jar and shake until the salt has dissolved. Add the oil and chives and shake again. Drain the potatoes, toss in some of the dressing and arrange half in the bottom of a 4 sturdy glass bowls, each about 500 ml (18 fl oz), or use a 2 litre (3½ pint) bowl.

4 Layer over the beans, then the tomatoes, the remaining potatoes and the eggs, drizzling a little of the dressing over each layer as you go. Finish with the lettuce and press down gently. Cover with clingfilm and chill until ready to use. Invert the salads on to plates and serve with the bread.

Experiment with the flavours in this dish. Arrange some criss-crossed anchovy fillets in the bottom of the bowl before adding the potatoes, then add a can of drained tuna in olive oil in between the cherry tomatoes, for a non-vegetarian option.

# Chickpea and spinach curry with flat bread

Nutrition notes per serving:
calories 589
protein 17 g
carbohydrate 68 g
fat 29 g
saturated fat 7 g
fibre 7 g
added sugar none
salt 2.18 g

Vegetarian dishes form a large part of the southern Indian diet, and this one is particularly tasty. Flat breads can literally be made in minutes, but don't be tempted to make them too far in advance, or they will begin to harden.

Preparation time: 20 minutes • Cooking time: 35 minutes • Serves 4

about 6 tablespoons sunflower oil
1 onion, thinly sliced
2 garlic cloves, crushed
2 tablespoons freshly grated root ginger
2 green chillies, seeded and finely chopped
2 tablespoons Madras curry powder
600 ml (1 pint) vegetable stock
a 200 g (7 oz) can chopped tomatoes
225 g (8 oz) baby new potatoes, halved

6 tablespoons thick Greek yoghurt
1 egg, lightly beaten
225 g (8 oz) self-raising flour, plus extra for dusting
2 tablespoons chopped fresh coriander
a 400 g (14 oz) can chickpeas, drained and rinsed
225 g (8 oz) baby spinach leaves
about 25 g (1 oz) butter
salt and freshly ground black pepper

1 Heat 2 tablespoons of oil in a pan with a lid and sauté the onion for 5 minutes until softened and lightly golden. Stir in the garlic, ginger and 1 of the chopped chillies and continue to cook for 1 minute. Add the curry powder, stock, tomatoes and potatoes, cover and simmer for 15–20 minutes until the potatoes are tender but still holding their shape.

2 Heat a large, non-stick frying-pan to make the flat breads. Mix 4 tablespoons of the yoghurt with enough warm water to make 120 ml (4 fl oz), then stir in the beaten egg. Put the flour into a bowl with half a teaspoon of salt. Make a well in the centre and add the yoghurt mixture, the remaining chilli and the coriander. Quickly mix to a soft but not sticky dough.

3 Turn the dough out on to a lightly floured work surface and knead gently for about 30 seconds until smooth. Divide into 4 portions then, using a rolling pin, roll out each piece to an oval shape about 5 mm (¼ inch) thick. Add a thin film of oil to the heated pan and cook the flatbreads for 4–5 minutes on each side until cooked through and lightly golden. Wrap in a clean tea towel to keep warm and repeat until you have 4 in total.

4 Add the chickpeas and spinach to the curry and cook for another few minutes until heated through, stirring occasionally. Stir in the remaining yoghurt until just warmed through. To serve, spread the warm flat breads with the butter. Divide the curry into warmed bowls set on plates with the buttered flat breads served on the side.

To make the dish even quicker, use parboiled potatoes and add them with the chickpeas and spinach in step 4.

Courgettes have a naturally high water content, which is why they must be squeezed dry before they are fried. This ensures that the fritters are lovely and crisp.

# Courgette, coriander and parmesan röstis

Nutrition notes per serving:
calories 552
protein 17 g
carbohydrate 25 g
fat 43 g
saturated fat 9 g
fibre 3 g
added sugar none
salt 0.85 g

Courgettes are such a versatile vegetable: here I've combined them with the freshness of lemon and the fragrance of coriander, and I'm sure these fritters will turn into a firm favourite.

Preparation time: 20 minutes • Cooking time: 15 minutes • Serves 4

550 g (1¼ lb) courgettes, coarsely grated
100 g (4 oz) ground rice
3 tablespoons shredded fresh coriander
  leaves
75 g (3 oz) Parmesan, freshly grated
1 egg, lightly beaten
1 teaspoon finely grated lemon rind
50 g (2 oz) flaked almonds

120 ml (4 fl oz)  olive oil
1 ripe tomato, seeded and finely diced
1 shallot, finely chopped
1 tablespoon lemon juice
100 g (4 oz) wild rocket or watercress,
  or a mixture of both
salt and freshly ground black pepper
lemon wedges, to garnish

1 Pre-heat the oven to 100°C/200°F/Gas ⅓/fan oven 80°C. Squeeze the courgettes dry in a clean tea towel and tip into a large bowl. Mix in the ground rice, coriander, Parmesan, egg, lemon rind and almonds. Season to taste and divide into 16 even-sized balls, then flatten slightly into patties.

2 Heat 2 tablespoons of the olive oil in a large, non-stick frying-pan and carefully add half of the patties. Cook for 2–3 minutes on each side or until cooked through, crisp and golden. Drain on kitchen paper and keep warm in the oven. Repeat with a further 2 tablespoons of oil and the remaining patties.

3 To make the dressing, place the remaining oil in a bowl and add the tomato, shallot and lemon juice, season to taste. Whisk until well combined. Divide the rocket or watercress or both among serving plates and drizzle over the dressing. Add the fritters and garnish with the lemon wedges to serve.

# Squash and pine nut risotto with rocket pesto

Nutrition notes per serving:
- calories 728
- protein 14 g
- carbohydrate 82 g
- fat 38 g
- saturated fat 14 g
- fibre 4 g
- added sugar none
- salt 0.56 g

This would be a great way to use up any leftover Roasted Butternut Squash and Root Vegetables (page 146). Simply heat them through and fold them into the risotto in place of the squash in step 4.

Preparation time: 10 minutes • Cooking time: 40–50 minutes • Serves 4

1 small butternut squash, peeled and cut into 2.5 cm (1 inch) cubes
about 120 ml (4 fl oz) olive oil
50 g (2 oz) pine nuts
4 tablespoons freshly grated Parmesan
50 g (2 oz) fresh rocket
1 litre (1¾ pints) vegetable stock

75 g (3 oz) unsalted butter
1 small onion, thinly sliced
2 garlic cloves, crushed
350 g (12 oz) Arborio (risotto) rice
150 ml (¼ pint) dry white wine
salt and freshly ground black pepper

1 Pre-heat the oven to 200°C/400°F/Gas 6/fan oven 180°C. Scatter the butternut squash cubes into a roasting tin and drizzle over 2 tablespoons of olive oil. Roast for 30–40 minutes or until tender, turning occasionally. Meanwhile, heat a frying-pan over a medium heat, add the pine nuts and cook for a few minutes, stirring occasionally. Set aside.

2 To make the rocket pesto, reserve 3 teaspoons of the Parmesan to use as a garnish and place the remaining Parmesan in a mini blender or liquidizer with 3–4 tablespoons of the remaining olive oil and the rocket. Blend briefly to combine – it should retain some texture (you don't want it to be too smooth). Season to taste, then transfer to a bowl, cover with clingfilm and chill until ready to use.

3 Pour the stock into a pan and bring up to a gentle simmer. Heat 2 tablespoons of olive oil and 50 g (2 oz) of the butter in another large pan. Add the onion and garlic and cook over a medium heat for 4–5 minutes until softened but not coloured, stirring occasionally. Increase the heat of the pan and add the rice, then cook for 1 minute, stirring continuously until the rice is opaque. Pour in the wine and allow to reduce until absorbed, stirring, then stir in a ladleful of stock and allow each stock addition to be almost completely absorbed before adding the next ladleful, until the rice is al dente – tender with a slight bite. This should take between 15–20 minutes.

4 Just before serving, stir in the remaining butter and the toasted pine nuts. Fold in the roasted butternut squash, season and divide among warmed, wide-rimmed serving bowls. Drizzle each with a little pesto and garnish with the reserved Parmesan. Serve immediately.

If you don't have a mini blender or liquidizer to make the pesto, finely chop the rocket using a large sharp knife, place in a small bowl and stir in the Parmesan and olive oil to combine.

Nutrition notes per serving:
calories 200
protein 10 g
carbohydrate 15 g
fat 11 g
saturated fat 2 g
fibre 3 g
added sugar 4 g
salt 0.68 g

# Huevos rancheros

These are baked eggs on a sea of spiced peppers and tomatoes, but I'm sure you like the original Mexican name, above. There are many variations of this dish, including one from Tunisia, which is called chakchouka and has no chilli.

Preparation time: 10 minutes • Cooking time: 25 minutes • Serves 4

1 tablespoon olive oil
1 large onion, chopped
2 garlic cloves, crushed
1 red and 1 yellow pepper, halved, seeded and sliced
1 red chilli, seeded and finely diced
1 teaspoon dried oregano

½ teaspoon ground cumin
1 tablespoon sugar
a 400 g (14 oz) can chopped tomatoes
4 eggs (preferably organic or free-range)
salt and freshly ground black pepper
fresh snipped chives, to garnish
fresh crusty bread, to serve

1  Pre-heat the oven to 180°C/350°F/Gas 4/fan oven 160°C. Heat the oil in a 28 cm (11 inch) ovenproof frying-pan. Tip in the onion, garlic, peppers and chilli and fry over a medium heat for 4–5 minutes until softened but not coloured, stirring occasionally. Stir in the oregano, cumin, sugar and the chopped tomatoes. Bring to a simmer, then cook for about 5 minutes until the peppers are completely tender and the sauce has slightly reduced and thickened. Season to taste.

2  Using the back of a wooden spoon, make 4 holes in the pepper mixture just large enough to fit the eggs, then carefully crack 1 into each hole. Season to taste and bake in the oven for 10–12 minutes or until the whites of the eggs are set but the yolks are still runny. Scatter over the chives to garnish and serve straight from the frying-pan to the table with plenty of crusty bread to mop up all the delicious juices. Have a great day!

# **low fat!** Baked tomatoes with puy lentils and goats' cheese

Nutrition notes per serving:
calories 227
protein 11 g
carbohydrate 17 g
fat 12 g
saturated fat 5 g
fibre 4 g
added sugar none
salt 1.59 g

For this recipe you can use many different types of lentils, including the red and brown varieties. I always keep a few cans of lentils in my store-cupboard as they really are handy and can be used in all manner of dishes.

Preparation time: 15 minutes • Cooking time: 10 minutes • Serves 4

4 ripe beef tomatoes
2 tablespoons olive oil, plus a little extra
 for greasing
1 small red onion, finely diced
2 garlic cloves, crushed
1 teaspoon plain flour
85 ml (3 fl oz) red wine
1 tablespoon tomato purée
1 teaspoon fresh thyme leaves

a 400 g (14 oz) can Puy lentils, drained
 and rinsed
1 tablespoon snipped fresh chives
3 tablespoons chopped fresh flat-leaf
 parsley, plus sprigs to garnish
85 g (3¼ oz) rindless goats' cheese,
 crumbled
salt and freshly ground black pepper
lightly dressed mixed salad, to serve

1  Pre-heat the oven to 190°C/375°F/Gas 5/fan oven 170°C. Slice the top off each tomato and discard. Being careful not to damage the outer skin, scoop out the seeds with a teaspoon, then turn the tomatoes upside down and set aside on kitchen paper for about 5 minutes to allow any excess juices to drain away. Place the tomatoes on a lightly greased baking sheet and roast for 10 minutes until slightly softened but still holding their shape.

2  Meanwhile, heat 1 tablespoon of oil in a large, non-stick pan and fry the onion and garlic for 2–3 minutes over a medium heat until softened but not coloured, stirring. Stir in the flour and continue to cook for another minute. Gradually add the wine, followed by the tomato purée and thyme, season to taste and simmer for 3 minutes until smooth and thickened, stirring occasionally.

3  Stir the lentils into the pan and heat through for 2 minutes, then remove from the heat and stir in the chives, parsley and goats' cheese. Remove the tomatoes from the oven and arrange on serving plates. Fill with the lentil mixture, drizzle over a little olive oil, garnish with parsley sprigs and serve immediately with a mixed salad.

If you can't get canned lentils, you can use any of the
dried varieties, but read the cooking instructions as
many involve overnight soaking or simmering for hours.

# Tagliatelle with roasted walnut and herb pesto

Nutrition notes per serving:
calories 577
protein 16 g
carbohydrate 67 g
fat 29 g
saturated fat 5 g
fibre 4 g
added sugar none
salt 0.47 g

This is a delicious and very speedy supper dish. It literally takes a few minutes to prepare, depending on how long your pasta takes to cook. Use any selection of soft herbs for the pesto and experiment with different types of nuts.

Preparation time: 10 minutes • Cooking time: 15 minutes • Serves 4

12 cherry tomatoes on the vine
50 g (2 oz) walnuts (shelled)
2 garlic cloves
6 tablespoons olive oil
350 g (12 oz) tagliatelle
2 tablespoons fresh chives, snipped

3 tablespoons chopped fresh flat-leaf parsley
4 tablespoons freshly grated or shaved Parmesan
salt and freshly ground black pepper

1 Pre-heat the oven to 220°C/425°F/Gas 7/fan oven 200°C. Snip the tomatoes into 4 bunches, then place in a shallow roasting tin with the walnuts and garlic cloves, and drizzle over a little olive oil – about 2 tablespoons. Season generously and roast for 10–12 minutes or until the tomatoes are starting to colour and the walnuts are toasted.

2 Meanwhile, cook the pasta in a large pan of boiling salted water for 8–10 minutes until al dente or according to the packet instructions.

3 Put the walnuts and garlic with any juices from the tin into a mini blender or liquidizer with the remaining oil. You can keep the tomatoes warm in the switched-off oven. Blitz the walnuts and garlic for a few seconds, then add the herbs and 2 tablespoons of the Parmesan. Pulse again briefly until just combined but not smooth. If you do not have a mini blender or liquidizer, finely chop all the ingredients for the pesto using a large sharp knife, or pound in a pestle and mortar.

4 Drain the pasta well and return to the pan, then fold in the pesto and season to taste. Serve with the roasted tomatoes on the side and a scattering of Parmesan cheese.

Why not make double the quantity of pesto and keep it to drizzle over bruschetta or grilled fish? If you store it in the fridge, it will keep for a couple of days.

# A bit
# the
# vegetables

# on side:
## and side orders

Wok-style pak choi ● Cheesy colcannon jackets ● Sweet Eddie cajun wedges ● Chilli and herb cajun cornbread ● Buttermilk soda scone swirls ● Onion marmalade ● Chilli ginger jam ● Roasted balsamic beetroot ● Roasted butternut squash and root vegetables ● French-style petit pois

Nutrition notes per serving:
calories 83
protein 3 g
carbohydrate 5 g
fat 6 g
saturated fat 0.7 g
fibre 0.3 g
added sugar 0.3 g
salt 1.61 g

# Wok-style pak choi

This is a very simple recipe and one of my favourite ways of preparing pak choi. It is excellent served with my Honey-glazed Duck with Sticky Rice (page 66) as it provides a lovely accompanying sauce.

Preparation time: 15 minutes • Cooking time: 15 minutes • Serves 4

2 tablespoons sunflower oil
6 salad onions, trimmed and cut into
  5 cm (2 inch) pieces on the diagonal
2 garlic cloves, crushed
a 2.5 cm (1 inch) piece fresh root ginger,
  peeled and cut into julienne (fine
  strips)

2 lemongrass stalks, outer leaves
  removed and cores finely chopped
1 red chilli, seeded and very thinly sliced
400 g (14 oz) pak choi, cut across into
  2.5 cm (1 inch) wide strips
1 tablespoon oyster sauce
1 tablespoon dark soy sauce

1 Heat the oil in a wok or deep, heavy-based frying-pan. Add the salad onions, garlic, ginger, lemongrass and chilli and stir-fry for 1 minute.

2 Add the pak choi to the wok and stir-fry for another minute, then sprinkle over a tablespoon of water, reduce the heat and steam-fry for another 2–3 minutes until lovely and tender.

3 Add the oyster sauce and soy sauce and toss together briefly until just combined. Tip into a warmed serving bowl and serve immediately.

If you want to ring the changes, you could try substituting Chinese cabbage or any other leafy green vegetable for the pak choi.

# low fat! Cheesy colcannon jackets

Nutrition notes per serving:
calories 282
protein 10 g
carbohydrate 39 g
fat 11 g
saturated fat 6 g
fibre 4 g
added sugar 0.2 g
salt 0.85 g

These cheesy colcannon jackets are fab on their own, or serve with grilled gammon steak, cooked with a honey and mustard glaze. You could also try adding some crispy chopped bacon to the mixture for an extra dimension.

Preparation time: 10 minutes • Cooking time: 55 minutes • Serves 4

4 x 200 g (7 oz) floury potatoes, such as
  King Edward or Desirée, scrubbed
25 g (1 oz) butter
225 g (8 oz) green cabbage (such as
  Savoy or York), finely shredded

2 salad onions, finely chopped
120 ml (4 fl oz) milk
2 teaspoons Dijon mustard
50 g (2 oz) mature Cheddar, grated
salt and freshly ground black pepper

1 Pre-heat the oven to 220°C/425°F/Gas 7/fan oven 200°C. Pierce the potatoes a couple of times to prevent them from splitting, then rub them with a little salt to help give an extra-crispy skin, and place directly on the shelf. Bake for about 45–50 minutes or until slightly softened when squeezed. Set aside until they are cool enough to handle.

2 Place a knob of the butter and a tablespoon of water in a pan with a tight-fitting lid over a high heat. Add the cabbage, salad onions and a pinch of salt. Cover, shake vigorously and cook for 1 minute. Shake again and cook for 1 minute until the cabbage is tender but still crisp.

3 Place the milk in a small pan and just bring to the boil, then remove from the heat. Cut each cooked potato in half lengthways, scoop out the flesh and quickly mash with the milk, remaining butter and the mustard. Beat with a wooden spoon until smooth, then mix in the cabbage, give it a good season and refill the potato shells.

4 Pre-heat the grill to medium. Arrange the colcannon jackets in a baking dish and sprinkle over the Cheddar, then flash under the grill until the cheese is bubbling and lightly browned. Serve at once.

Colcannon was traditionally made in Ireland at
Hallowe'en. A lucky charm was wrapped and tucked in
the centre for someone to find. Ooh – just like Christmas!

# Sweet eddie cajun wedges

Nutrition notes per serving:
calories 602
protein 8 g
carbohydrate 68 g
fat 35 g
saturated fat 16 g
fibre 6 g
added sugar none
salt 0.88 g

Whenever we are having a party I always make trays of these wedges. They're always a winner and, dare I say it, cheap as chips. I normally cook them in advance and then just re-heat them as they're needed.

Preparation time: 10 minutes • Cooking time: 1 hour • Serves 4–6

4 x 175 g (6 oz) potatoes
4 x 175 g (6 oz) orange-fleshed sweet
  potatoes
4 tablespoons olive oil
1–2 tablespoons Cajun seasoning
  (see tip)

125 g (4½ oz) cream cheese
150 ml (¼ pint) soured cream
8 sun-blushed (see page 69) tomatoes,
  chopped
4 tablespoons snipped fresh chives
salt and freshly ground black pepper

1 Pre-heat the oven to 200°C/400°F/Gas 6/fan oven 180°C. Scrub the potatoes and sweet potatoes and cut each one into 6 even-sized wedges. Place the potatoes in a pan of boiling water, return to the boil and blanch for 2–3 minutes, then quickly drain. Put the olive oil in a large roasting tin with a teaspoon of salt and the Cajun seasoning to taste. Add the wedges and toss until they are all well coated in the flavoured oil, then arrange them in rows 'sitting' upright on their skins. Bake for 35–40 minutes until completely tender and lightly golden, with an extra 10–15 minutes if you like them really crunchy.

2 To make the dip, place the cream cheese, soured cream and sun-blushed tomatoes in a food processor or liquidizer and blitz to combine. Transfer to a serving bowl, stir in the chives and season to taste. Cover with clingfilm and chill until ready to use – the longer the better to allow the flavours to mingle. More mingle, more flavour.

3 If you don't want to serve the Cajun wedges immediately, allow them to cool and chill for up to 24 hours covered with clingfilm, then re-heat in the oven for 15–20 minutes until piping hot. Otherwise, pile them onto a large, warmed serving platter and serve with the sun-blushed tomato and soured cream dip.

It's worth splashing out on a good quality Cajun seasoning. There are now some excellent brands around. Look out for the ones sold in small foil packets, which are incredibly pungent.

Cultured buttermilk is now available from all large supermarkets. You'll find it in cartons in the chilled section.

# Chilli and herb cajun cornbread

Nutrition notes per serving:
calories 454
protein 14 g
carbohydrate 68 g
fat 16 g
saturated fat 8 g
fibre 2 g
added sugar 4 g
salt 2.8 g

This is my version of an all-American classic. Obviously, it tastes best warm, not long out of the oven, but it can be made up to 1 day in advance and stored in an airtight container at room temperature.

Preparation time: 15 minutes • Cooking time: 50 minutes • Serves 4–6

50 g (2 oz) butter, plus extra for serving
150 g (5 oz) self-raising flour
1 teaspoon salt
2 teaspoons baking powder
1 tablespoon caster sugar
½ teaspoon cracked black pepper
150 g (5 oz) yellow cornmeal
  (maizemeal)

2 eggs, lightly beaten
300 ml (½ pint) cultured buttermilk
1 red chilli, seeded and finely chopped
2 tablespoons chopped fresh mixed
  herbs (such as flat-leaf parsley, chives
  and basil)

1 Pre-heat the oven to 180°C/350°F/Gas 4/fan oven 160°C. Melt the butter in a small pan or in the microwave and use 1 tablespoon to grease a 1.2 litre (2 pint) non-stick loaf tin. Set the remainder aside. Sift the flour, salt and baking powder into a bowl, then tip in the sugar, pepper and cornmeal and give it a good mix.

2 Make a well in the centre of the dry ingredients and quickly stir in the eggs, buttermilk and remaining butter until you have achieved a smooth, thick batter. Fold in the chilli and herbs until just combined. Spoon the mixture into the prepared tin and bake for 40–45 minutes or until golden brown and an inserted skewer comes out clean.

3 Using a clean tea towel, carefully remove the loaf from the tin onto a wire rack, then leave to cool. Serve the loaf, warm or cold, sliced with butter.

# Buttermilk soda scone swirls

Nutrition notes per serving:
calories 566
protein 19 g
carbohydrate 89 g
fat 17 g
saturated fat 6 g
fibre 4 g
added sugar none
salt 2.83 g

These delicious scone swirls are best eaten as soon as they are cool enough to handle. If you want to keep them any longer, sprinkle over a little water as soon as they are out of the tin and wrap in a tea towel to stop the crust becoming too hard.

Preparation time: 15 minutes • Cooking time: 40 minutes • Serves 4–6

450 g (1 lb) self-raising flour, plus extra for dusting
1 teaspoon salt
1 teaspoon baking powder
25 g (1 oz) unsalted butter, plus extra for greasing and serving
300 ml (½ pint) cultured buttermilk

2 eggs, lightly beaten
about 4 tablespoons sun-dried tomato paste
2 tablespoons chopped fresh mixed herbs (such as flat-leaf parsley, chives and basil)
25 g (1 oz) freshly grated Parmesan

1 Pre-heat the oven to 220°C/425°F/Gas 7/fan oven 200°C. Grease a 23 cm (9 inch) non-stick spring-form cake tin and line the base with non-stick baking paper. Sift the flour, salt and baking powder into a bowl and rub in the butter using your fingers. Make a well in the centre, then pour in the buttermilk and half of the beaten eggs. Using a large metal spoon, quickly but gently mix the liquid into the flour until you have achieved a soft, but not sticky, dough, adding a little warm water if necessary.

2 Turn the dough out on to a lightly floured work surface and knead lightly for 30 seconds, then roll out gently to a rectangle that measures about 35.5 x 25 cm (14 x 10 inches). Spread over the sun-dried tomato paste and scatter over the herbs and grated Parmesan. Roll up from the short end (as you would for a Swiss roll) then cut into 3 cm (1½ inch) slices and place them side-by-side in the prepared tin, allowing them enough room to swell together.

3 Use the remaining egg to brush all over the swirls. Bake for 15 minutes, then reduce the oven temperature to 200°C/400°F/Gas 6/fan oven 180°C and bake for another 20–25 minutes or until well risen and golden brown. Leave in the tin for 5 minutes, then release and transfer to a wire rack and allow to cool a little. Arrange on a serving platter and serve at once with butter to spread.

**VARIATIONS**

**Herby:** add 3 tablespoons of chopped fresh mixed herbs (such as parsley, chives and basil) to the scone mixture and replace the herbs in the filling with two finely chopped salad onions.

**Cheese and onion:** replace the sun-dried tomato paste with ordinary tomato purée; the herbs with finely chopped onion and the Parmesan with Cheddar.

**Pesto and mushroom:** use basil pesto and scatter over 100 g (4 oz) of finely chopped chestnut mushrooms that have been sautéed in butter until tender.

**low fat!**

Nutrition notes per 25 ml tablespoonful:
calories 44
protein 0.6 g
carbohydrate 6 g
fat 2 g
saturated fat 0.3 g
fibre 0.5 g
added sugar 3 g
salt 0.06 g

# Onion marmalade

This onion marmalade can be used in so many different ways. If it is stored in sterilized jars it will last for up to 2 months. I find it a useful staple to keep in the fridge as it is delicious with cold meats, in pies ... I could go on and on.

Preparation time: 10 minutes • Cooking time: 50 minutes • Makes about 450 ml (¾ pint)

3 large onions, thinly sliced
3 garlic cloves, thinly sliced
3 tablespoons olive oil
1 teaspoon black mustard seeds

1 teaspoon coriander seeds
3 tablespoons red wine vinegar
4 tablespoons dark muscovado sugar
salt and freshly ground black pepper

1 Tip the onions into a large, heavy-based pan and add the garlic, olive oil, mustard and coriander seeds. Stir well to combine and then cook gently over a low heat for 20 minutes, stirring occasionally.

2 Stir in the vinegar and sugar and continue to cook for another 10–20 minutes until the onions have become completely translucent and the marmalade well reduced, stirring occasionally. Stir in 4 tablespoons of water and continue to cook for another 10 minutes until the marmalade is well thickened and slightly sticky. Season to taste.

3 If you are not planning on using the onion marmalade immediately, wash a Kilner jar or a couple of jam jars, rinse thoroughly, then dry in a warm oven. Stand them upside down on a clean tea towel.

4 If you are using jam jars, fill them, then cover the marmalade with a disc of waxed paper while still hot or else completely cold, then seal with a dampened disc of clear plastic, secure with an elastic band and screw back on their tops. Simply secure and close a Kilner jar in the normal way. Label and store in a cool, dark place for up to 2 months, then use as required. Otherwise transfer the marmalade into a serving bowl, cover with clingfilm and chill until needed.

I sometimes use this marmalade as a base for a tart.
Spread a few tablespoonfuls over a circle of puff pastry
and top with goats' cheese, prosciutto and figs – yummy!

Nutrition notes per 25 ml tablespoonful:
calories 29
protein 0.3 g
carbohydrate 5 g
fat 1 g
saturated fat 0.1 g
fibre 0.2 g
added sugar 3.4 g
salt 0.11 g

# Chilli ginger jam

This is one of my store-cupboard essentials that's simple to make, and is the ideal substitute for sweet chilli sauce when making the Sweet Chilli Tomato Tarte Tatin (page 28) or as a dip with the Crispy Chilli Orange Grilled Chicken (page 78).

Preparation time: 15 minutes • Cooking time: 8 minutes • Makes about 300 ml (½ pint)

1 tablespoon sunflower oil
1 onion, finely chopped
2 garlic cloves, crushed
3 red chillies, seeded and finely chopped
1 tablespoon grated, fresh root ginger
juice of 1 lime

finely grated rind and juice of 1 orange
3 tablespoons clear honey
1 tablespoon malt vinegar
2 tablespoons tomato ketchup

1 Heat the oil in a small pan and fry the onion and garlic over a moderate heat for 2 minutes until softened but not coloured, stirring. Add the chillies and ginger and then continue to cook for another 2 minutes, stirring occasionally.

2 Squeeze in the lime juice with the orange rind and juice, honey, vinegar and ketchup. Slowly bring to a gentle simmer and then cook for another 2 minutes to allow the flavours to combine, stirring occasionally. Remove from the heat and allow to cool completely. Transfer to a bowl, cover with clingfilm and chill until needed.

Try the jam in sandwiches, or add a spoonful to your favourite stir-fry. It could soon become a store-cupboard favourite of yours, too.

# **low fat!** Roasted balsamic beetroot

Nutrition notes per serving:
  calories 173
  protein 4 g
  carbohydrate 14 g
  fat 11 g
  saturated fat 4 g
  fibre 3 g
  added sugar none
  salt 0.56 g

Beetroot just seems to get forgotten about all too often. Try this recipe as an alternative vegetable with your Sunday roast, or even to liven up some leftover beef along with handfuls of watercress for a quick and easy salad.

Preparation time: 10 minutes • Cooking time: 25–30 minutes • Serves 4

6 large raw beetroot
3 tablespoons balsamic vinegar
1 teaspoon cumin seeds
2 tablespoons olive oil

150 ml (¼ pint) half-fat crème fraîche
2 tablespoons freshly grated horseradish
  (from a jar is fine)
salt and freshly ground black pepper

1  Pre-heat the oven to 200°C/400°F/Gas 6/fan oven 180°C. Peel the beetroot and cut each one into 6–8 wedges. Tip into a roasting tin, drizzle over the vinegar, sprinkle the cumin seeds on top and season generously, then drizzle over the oil. Roast for 25–30 minutes until tender but retaining a bit of bite, turning occasionally.

2  To make the horseradish crème fraîche, place the crème fraîche in a bowl and beat in the horseradish; season to taste. Spoon the roasted beetroot into a warmed serving dish and serve immediately or at room temperature with the horseradish crème fraîche.

You could also try allowing the beetroot to cool, adding some orange segments or smoked mackerel and using the horseradish crème fraîche as a dressing.

# low fat! Roasted butternut squash and root vegetables

Nutrition notes per serving:
- calories 230
- protein 5 g
- carbohydrate 33 g
- fat 10 g
- saturated fat 1 g
- fibre 9 g
- added sugar none
- salt 0.35 g

These roasted veggies are delicious served hot or at room temperature. You could substitute sweet potato or beetroot for any of the vegetables in this recipe, while the rosemary could be exchanged for thyme.

Preparation time: 15 minutes • Cooking time: 35–40 minutes • Serves 4–6

1 small butternut squash, cut into slices, each about 1 cm (½ inch) thick
2 large carrots, cut into quarters
2 small parsnips, cut into quarters
2 small white turnips, cut into quarters
1 red onion, cut into 6 wedges
4 garlic cloves, peeled
4 fresh rosemary sprigs
1 lemon, cut into wedges
3 tablespoons olive oil
salt and freshly ground black pepper

1 Pre-heat the oven to 200°C/400°F/Gas 6/fan oven 180°C. Tip the butternut squash, vegetables and garlic into a large roasting tin – you may need to use two. Add the rosemary sprigs and lemon wedges and then drizzle the olive oil on top, tossing to coat.

2 Season generously and roast for 35–40 minutes or until the vegetables are just tender and lightly charred, tossing occasionally. Spoon into a serving dish and serve immediately or at room temperature.

I like to serve these with a simply grilled fish. You could also use them instead of the squash in the Squash and Pine Nut Risotto (page 120).

# **low fat!** French-style petits pois

Nutrition notes per serving:
calories 162
protein 8 g
carbohydrate 7 g
fat 11 g
saturated fat 5 g
fibre 3 g
added sugar none
salt 1.10 g

The traditional way of cooking French-style peas is to layer lettuce in the bottom of a pan, top with peas and white wine, then steam for about 10 minutes before whisking in cold butter. Every cook has their own variation – this is mine.

Preparation time: 5 minutes • Cooking time: 10 minutes • Serves 4

225 g (8 oz) frozen petits pois or
  garden peas
1 fresh mint sprig, plus 1 tablespoon
  chopped fresh mint
25 g (1 oz) unsalted butter
3 salad onions, trimmed and thinly sliced
75 g (3 oz) pancetta cubes (cubetti)

1 tablespoon plain flour
3 tablespoons dry white wine
6 tablespoons chicken stock
1 teaspoon prepared English mustard
1 Little Gem lettuce or a few Iceberg
  lettuce leaves, shredded
salt and freshly ground black pepper

1 Cook the petits pois or peas in a pan of boiling salted water with the mint sprig for 3 minutes or according to the packet instructions, then drain and quickly refresh. Melt the butter in a separate pan and fry the salad onions and pancetta over a moderate heat for 2–3 minutes, until the pancetta is sizzling and lightly golden, stirring occasionally.

2 Stir in the flour and continue to cook for another minute, then gradually add the wine and stock, stirring until smooth after each addition. Bring to the boil, then reduce the heat and simmer gently for 2–3 minutes until thickened and smooth.

3 Add the mustard, chopped mint, lettuce and refreshed petits pois. Cook gently to just heat through, allowing the lettuce to wilt slightly, stirring occasionally. Season to taste, tip into a warmed serving dish and serve immediately.

This dish is always a winner with family and friends and is a great way of jazzing up that great freezer standby, frozen peas or petit pois.

# Perfect

# puds

Double chocolate croissant pudding with bourbon • Coconut carrot cake with rosemary cream • Dreamy chocolate hazelnut torte • Banana tarte tatin • Warm mascarpone berry spring rolls • Eton mess with maddie maltesers • Clare's chocolate, coffee and cardamom mousse • Easy baileys crème brûlée • Orange-flower, yoghurt and pistachio pudding • Pineapple, ginger and coconut sabayon

# Double chocolate croissant pudding with bourbon

Nutrition notes per serving:
* calories 1017
* protein 14 g
* carbohydrate 85 g
* fat 69 g
* saturated fat 29 g
* fibre 1 g
* added sugar 56 g
* salt 0.81 g

This delightful, rich, chocolate pudding always goes down a treat, and even if you're watching the calories a little goes a long way …

Preparation time: 20 minutes • Cooking time: 40 minutes • Serves 6–8

25 g (1 oz) pecan nuts
4 large, good-quality croissants, 1 day old (no more than 300 g/10 oz in total)
50 g (2 oz) plain chocolate, finely chopped
450 ml (¾ pint) milk
450 ml (¾ pint) double cream

4 egg yolks
150 g (5 oz) golden caster sugar
225 g (8 oz) white chocolate, finely chopped
about 4 tablespoons bourbon
4 tablespoons apricot jam
vanilla ice-cream or lightly whipped cream, to serve

1 Pre-heat the oven to 180°C/350°F/Gas 4/fan oven 160°C. Toast the pecans in a small, heavy-based frying-pan over a medium heat; remove from the heat. Cut the croissants into 5 mm (¼ inch) slices and layer in a large ovenproof dish (about 35 x 23 cm/ 14 x 9 inches). Roughly chop the pecan nuts and scatter on top along with the plain chocolate.

2 Place the milk and cream in a pan and just bring to the boil. Using an electric mixer or hand whisk, beat the egg yolks and sugar in a bowl until pale and thickened. Slowly whisk in the heated milk mixture and then stir in the white chocolate until melted – you may need to place this over a pan of simmering water if the mixture has cooled down too much. Stir in enough of the bourbon to taste.

3 Pour the egg mixture over the croissants. Cover tightly with tin foil and set aside for 10 minutes to allow the croissants to soak up the custard. Bake for 25–30 minutes until just set but with a slight wobble in the middle. Remove the tin foil and discard.

4 Pre-heat the grill to medium. Heat the apricot jam in a small pan or the microwave and when syrupy use to brush all over the top of the pudding. Flash the pudding under the grill for 2–3 minutes until bubbling and lightly golden (or use a blow torch – see tip). Serve warm or at room temperature with vanilla ice-cream or lightly whipped cream – mmm … both!

I use a cook's blow torch at home to caramelize the top
of puddings – you'll find them in all good kitchen shops.

# Coconut carrot cake with rosemary cream

Nutrition notes per serving:
★ calories 753
★ protein 9 g
★ carbohydrate 63 g
★ fat 53 g
★ saturated fat 18 g
★ fibre 4 g
★ added sugar 32 g
★ salt 0.38 g

You can't beat a tasty carrot cake – just ask my kids …
For perfect presentation, dip tiny fresh rosemary sprigs into lightly beaten egg white. Shake off any excess and then coat in caster sugar. Leave to dry and use to decorate the cream.

Preparation time: 20 minutes • Cooking time: 35 minutes • Serves 6

150 ml (¼ pint) sunflower oil
2 eggs
175 g (6 oz) light muscovado sugar
finely grated rind and juice of 1 orange
225 g (8 oz) carrots, coarsely grated
75 g (3 oz) shredded coconut
50 g (2 oz) walnuts, chopped
50 g (2 oz) raisins

75 g (3 oz) self-raising wholemeal flour
75 g (3 oz) self-raising flour
1 teaspoon baking powder
½ teaspoon ground cinnamon
a pinch of freshly grated nutmeg
1 tablespoon caster sugar
1 small fresh rosemary sprig
300 ml (½ pint) crème fraîche

1  Pre-heat the oven to 180°C/350°F/Gas 4/fan oven 160°C. Grease 6 x 120 ml (4 fl oz) ramekins, then cut 6 lengths of non-stick baking paper and roll into 7.5 cm (3 inch) high cylinders. Use to line the ramekins and then cut out circles to line the bases; secure the sides of the paper cylinders with string tied in a bow. Arrange on a baking sheet and set aside.

2  Place the oil in a food processor with the eggs, sugar and orange rind, then blitz until blended. Place the carrots, coconut, walnuts and raisins in a large bowl and stir in the oil mixture. Sift in the flours, baking powder and spices, then fold in until just combined. Divide the mixture among the lined ramekins and bake on the baking sheet for 30–35 minutes or until well risen and an inserted skewer comes out clean.

3  Meanwhile, make the rosemary cream. Place the orange juice in a small pan with the caster sugar and rosemary, then simmer over a medium heat until reduced by half. Remove from the heat, and leave to cool down. When cool, remove the rosemary sprig and discard. Fold into the crème fraîche, then cover and chill until ready to use.

4  Leave the cooked carrot cakes to cool in the ramekins for about 5 minutes, then turn them out on to serving plates, tearing off the baking paper. Serve with a dollop of rosemary cream.

Instead of individual cakes, you could use the same quantity of mixture to fill a 900 ml (1½ pint) loaf tin, lined with non-stick baking paper. Bake in a pre-heated oven at 160°C/325°F/Gas 3/fan oven 140°C, for 1 hour.

# Dreamy chocolate hazelnut torte

Nutrition notes per serving:
★ calories 573
★ protein 10 g
★ carbohydrate 39 g
★ fat 43 g
★ saturated fat 17 g
★ fibre 2 g
★ added sugar 38 g
★ salt 0.17 g

Good chocolate really brings this dessert to life with its velvety texture. The same could be said of the red-fruit compote – there's now a wide range to choose from. In summer, try serving the torte with a selection of fresh berries.

Preparation time: 15 minutes • Cooking time: 50 minutes • Serves 8

175 g (6 oz) unsalted butter, plus extra for greasing
175 g (6 oz) blanched hazelnuts
175 g (6 oz) plain chocolate, broken into pieces (about 70% cocoa solids)

175 g (6 oz) golden caster sugar
6 eggs, separated
red-fruit compote and vanilla ice-cream, to serve
icing sugar, to decorate

1 Pre-heat the oven to 180°C/350°F/Gas 4/fan oven 160°C. Lightly grease a 23 cm (9 inch) non-stick spring-form cake tin that is no more than 7.5 cm (3 inches) deep and line the base with non-stick baking paper. Place the hazelnuts in a roasting tin and roast for 10 minutes until toasted but not burnt. Leave to cool a little, then blitz in a food processor for 30 seconds until finely ground.

2 Place the chocolate in a heatproof bowl set over a pan of simmering water and allow to melt, remove the bowl from the pan and set aside to cool a little. Place half of the sugar and the butter into a large bowl and, using an electric mixer or hand whisk, beat together until pale and creamy. Beat in the egg yolks and melted chocolate.

3 Wash the beaters then whisk the egg whites in a separate bowl until you have achieved soft peaks, then add the remaining sugar and whisk again until nice and stiff. Fold in the ground hazelnuts, then gently fold into the chocolate mixture in two or three batches (to keep the air in). Spoon into the prepared tin and bake for 40–45 minutes or until a skewer pushed into the centre of the cake comes out clean.

4 Remove the cake from the oven and leave to cool in the tin, then cut into slices and arrange on serving plates with the red-fruit compote and scoops of vanilla ice-cream. Decorate with a light dusting of icing sugar and serve at once.

You can keep the torte for up to 4 days in the fridge –
I'd even say it improves with time. Enjoy!

# Banana tarte tatin

Nutrition notes per serving:
- calories 526
- protein 4 g
- carbohydrate 75 g
- fat 23 g
- saturated fat 12 g
- fibre 1 g
- added sugar 31 g
- salt 0.31 g

Hot or cold, this dessert is a knockout! You can make it several hours in advance and leave it to cool. This gives all the juices time to be well absorbed into the bananas and allows the caramel to set slightly.

Preparation time: 15 minutes • Cooking time: 35 minutes • Serves 6

100 g (4 oz) unsalted butter
175 g (6 oz) caster sugar
6 large bananas
juice of 1 lime
4 tablespoons light rum

¼ teaspoon ground allspice
225 g (8 oz) ready-made puff pastry,
  thawed if frozen
plain flour, for dusting
clotted cream or crème fraîche, to serve

1 Pre-heat the oven to 200°C/400°F/Gas 6/fan oven 180°C. Melt the butter in a 20–23 cm (8–9 inch) heavy-based ovenproof frying-pan with the sugar until the sugar has dissolved, stirring occasionally. Continue to cook for 2–3 minutes or until the mixture is a golden caramel colour, stirring continuously.

2 Peel the bananas and cut into thick slices, then toss them in half of the lime juice. Add the rum to the sugar mixture with the remaining lime juice and allspice and allow to bubble down, stirring to combine. Tip in the bananas and toss until they are evenly coated.

3 Meanwhile, roll out the pastry on a lightly floured surface into a round 2.5 cm (1 inch) larger than the frying-pan. Lay over the top of the bananas, tucking in the edges and turning them down so that when the tarte is turned out, the edges will create a rim that will hold in the caramel and banana juices. Bake for 20–25 minutes, or until the pastry is puffed up and golden brown.

4 Leave the tarte in the tin for a minute or two, then loosen the edges with a round-bladed knife and carefully turn upside down on to a flat serving plate. Rearrange any bananas that have loosened, cut into slices and transfer to warmed serving plates. Add a spoonful of clotted cream or crème fraîche to serve.

If you don't have the correct sized ovenproof frying-pan, start the tarte off in an ordinary frying-pan or wok and transfer to a shallow 23 cm (9 inch) cake tin to finish cooking.

# Warm mascarpone berry spring rolls

Nutrition notes per serving:
★ calories 705
★ protein 7 g
★ carbohydrate 56 g
★ fat 52 g
★ saturated fat 32 g
★ fibre 0.9 g
★ added sugar 12 g
★ salt 1.22 g

I always use authentic Greek filo pastry, as it makes all the difference. The inspiration for this dessert came from a well-known restaurant in New York where I was given something similar as an unusual alternative to petits fours.

Preparation time: 15 minutes • Cooking time: 15 minutes • Serves 4

250 g (9 oz) mascarpone cheese
finely grated rind of 1 lemon
2 tablespoons sifted icing sugar, plus
  extra for dusting
100 g (4 oz) unsalted butter
275 g (10 oz) filo pastry, thawed
  if frozen

150 g (5 oz) mixed small berries, such as
  raspberries, blueberries, stoned
  cherries and/or blackberries
vanilla ice-cream, to serve

1  Pre-heat the oven to 220°C/425°F/Gas 7/fan oven 200°C. Place the mascarpone in a bowl and beat in the lemon rind and icing sugar. Melt the butter in a small pan or in the microwave, then remove from the heat and allow to cool a little.

2  Cut the filo pastry into 25 cm (10 inch) squares, then layer up three squares, lightly brushing with melted butter between each layer and keeping the rest of the pastry covered with a damp tea towel while you work.

3  Spoon a quarter of the mascarpone mixture about 7.5 cm (3 inches) away from one of the corners and scatter a quarter of the berries on top. Pull over the corner to enclose the filling completely, then fold in the two sides and roll up like a cigar. Brush all over with melted butter and place on a non-stick baking sheet. Repeat with the remaining pastry and filling until you have 4 rolls in total. Give the spring rolls a quick chill to allow the butter to firm up, but not too long or the filo is in danger of drying out.

4  Bake the spring rolls for 10–12 minutes or until the pastry is cooked through and golden brown. Pop a spring roll on to a warmed serving plate, dust with icing sugar and serve with vanilla ice-cream.

Fresh or frozen berries would work well in this dish.
There's now a fantastic selection of frozen mixed-berry
packs available in supermarkets.

# Eton mess with
# maddie maltesers

Nutrition notes per serving:
- calories 530
- protein 5 g
- carbohydrate 44 g
- fat 38 g
- saturated fat 24 g
- fibre 2 g
- added sugar 39 g
- salt 0.18 g

This dessert is a family favourite in my house. The kids also get to help and have fun smashing up the meringues and Maltesers. If it's for adults only, you could add a splash of cassis or your favourite liqueur to the raspberries.

Preparation time: 15 minutes • Cooking time: none • Serves 4

300 ml (½ pint) double cream
about 50 g (2 oz) caster sugar, plus
 extra, if the berries are tart
250 g (9 oz) fresh raspberries
2 meringue nests, about 75 g (3 oz)
 in weight

a 40 g (1½ oz) packet Maltesers
4 fresh mint sprigs, to decorate
 (optional)
icing sugar, to dust

1 Whisk the cream with 1 tablespoon of the sugar in a bowl, using a balloon whisk or an electric beater, until soft peaks form. Be careful if you're using electric beaters, as this will happen really fast.

2 Place the raspberries in a separate bowl with the remaining sugar and, using a fork, lightly crush – you may need to add some extra sugar if the raspberries are particularly tart or if you have a very sweet tooth.

3 Lightly crush the meringues and the Maltesers. I find this easiest to do while they are still in the packet, as there's less mess. Don't over-mix here, but gently fold the raspberries into the cream with the crushed meringue and Maltesers, until you get a rippled effect. Spoon the mixture into serving glasses set on plates, decorate with mint sprigs, if you like, and dust with icing sugar. Serve immediately.

You could use any soft berries for this recipe –
strawberries, blackberries, redcurrants, or a combination.

# low fat! Clare's chocolate, coffee and cardamom mousse

Nutrition notes per serving:
- calories 235
- protein 5 g
- carbohydrate 29 g
- fat 12 g
- saturated fat 6 g
- fibre 0.8 g
- added sugar 28 g
- salt 0.10 g

My wife Clare calls this 'spread-it-on-me-thighs mousse'! It's rich, light and fluffy ... but amazingly it's low in fat! Good-quality chocolate makes all the difference, so try to get chocolate with a minimum of 50% cocoa solids. Mmm.

Preparation time: 15 minutes + chilling time • Cooking time: 3 minutes • Serves 4

130 g (4¾ oz) plain chocolate, plus extra for grating
85 ml (3 fl oz) cold strong black coffee (espresso is great)
2 cardamom pods, husks discarded and seeds lightly crushed

2 eggs, separated
2 tablespoons caster sugar
crème fraîche and grated chocolate, to serve, optional

1  Place 4 x 120 ml (4 fl oz) ramekins or serving glasses in the fridge; this will help the mousses to set quickly.

2  Break the chocolate into chunks, then put in a large heatproof bowl with the coffee and cardamom seeds. Set over a pan of simmering water for about 3 minutes until the chocolate has melted, stirring occasionally with a wooden spoon and making sure that the bowl is not touching the hot water. Remove from the heat and set aside to cool slightly.

3  Once the chocolate has cooled for a few minutes, beat in the egg yolks one at a time, using a wooden spoon. Place the egg whites in a separate bowl and, using a balloon whisk or an electric beater, whisk to soft peaks. Tip the sugar into the stiff whites and continue to whisk until the mixture is glossy and meringue-like.

4  Stir a spoonful of the whites into the melted chocolate – this helps to loosen the mixture – then carefully and lightly fold in the rest of the meringue. Spoon the mixture into the chilled ramekins or glasses and chill for at least 40 minutes (or up to 2 hours if time allows). Serve on plates with a good dollop of crème fraîche topped with a little grated chocolate, if liked.

# Easy baileys crème brûlée

Nutrition notes per serving:
- calories 632
- protein 6 g
- carbohydrate 33 g
- fat 51 g
- saturated fat 25 g
- fibre 0.8 g
- added sugar 29 g
- salt 0.54 g

It's always nice to produce a quick and simple version of a classic dessert. You can try using different types of nuts in this, such as crushed pecans or pistachios. Whip your cream lightly, as the alcohol in the Baileys will slightly thicken it anyway.

Preparation time: 10 minutes • Cooking time: 1 minute • Serves 4

300 ml (½ pint) double cream
6 tablespoons caster sugar (golden, if possible)
150 ml (¼ pint) thick Greek yoghurt

6 tablespoons Baileys Irish Cream
1 tablespoon vanilla-bean paste or 1 vanilla bean split and scraped
50 g (2 oz) toasted hazelnuts, chopped

1 Whip the cream and 2 tablespoons of the sugar in a large bowl using a balloon whisk or electric beater, until it is the consistency of the Greek yoghurt. Fold in the yoghurt, using a large metal spoon, then mix in the Baileys Irish Cream, vanilla-bean paste and the hazelnuts until well combined.

2 Divide the cream mixture among 4 x 150 ml (¼ pint) ramekins, levelling down the tops, and then sprinkle about a tablespoon of sugar evenly over each one, completely covering the cream.

3 Pre-heat the grill to high. Arrange on a sturdy baking sheet and place under the hot grill for 30 seconds or until the sugar has just melted – you could also use a blow torch for this if you have one. Allow the sugar to cool and set for a minute or so before serving.

You can make these brûlées in advance, but don't put the sugar topping on until about 30 minutes before you're ready to serve.

# Orange-flower, yoghurt and pistachio pudding

Nutrition notes per serving:
- ★ calories 302
- ★ protein 13 g
- ★ carbohydrate 26 g
- ★ fat 17 g
- ★ saturated fat 6 g
- ★ fibre 0.1 g
- ★ added sugar 20 g
- ★ salt 0.30 g

For a beautiful, light pudding with a gorgeous moist base this is one recipe you have to try. Orange-flower water is available from most large supermarkets or from specialist food stores; it has a wonderfully fragrant flavour.

Preparation time: 20 minutes • Cooking time: 35 minutes • Serves 4

3 eggs, separated
75 g (3 oz) caster sugar
1 tablespoon plain flour
1 tablespoon orange-flower water
grated rind and juice of 1 lemon

300 ml (½ pint) thick Greek yoghurt
40 g (1½ oz) shelled unsalted pistachio
  nuts, roughly chopped
crème fraîche or vanilla ice-cream, to
  serve

1 Pre-heat the oven to 160°C/325°F/Gas 3/fan oven 140°C. Grease and line a 23 cm (9 inch) spring-form cake tin. Place the egg yolks and sugar in a large bowl and, using an electric beater or wooden spoon, beat until pale and fluffy. Fold in the flour, orange-flower water, lemon rind and juice until well combined. Finally stir in the yoghurt and half of the pistachio nuts.

2 Whisk the egg whites in a separate large bowl until stiff peaks form. Stir 1 spoonful of beaten egg whites into the yoghurt mixture to loosen it, then gently fold in the remaining egg white, being careful not to knock out too much air.

3 Spoon the mixture into the prepared cake tin, and place in the centre of the oven and bake for 20 minutes. Remove from the oven and sprinkle over the remaining pistachio nuts, increase the heat to 180°C/350°F/Gas 4/fan oven 160°C and cook for another 15 minutes until the pudding has risen and is golden brown.

4 Take the pudding out of the oven and leave to cool for about 5 minutes – don't worry if it sinks slightly, as that's supposed to happen. Spoon the warm pudding on to plates, and serve with a dollop of crème fraîche or vanilla ice-cream.

For an extra special touch, stir a splash of vanilla extract into some Greek yoghurt and serve with the pudding.

The fruit for this dish can be prepared in advance, but the sabayon needs to be made just before you serve it — it only takes a few minutes.

# Pineapple, ginger and coconut sabayon

Nutrition notes per serving:
- calories 269
- protein 3 g
- carbohydrate 42 g
- fat 10 g
- saturated fat 5 g
- fibre 2 g
- added sugar 20 g
- salt 0.08 g

This is an incredibly versatile recipe that's speedy and yummy and can be made using virtually any fruit that is in season. Combine the fruit with basic store-cupboard ingredients and you have the perfect emergency dessert.

Preparation time: 10 minutes • Cooking time: 10 minutes • Serves 4

1 ripe pineapple, peeled, cut into slices and the core removed
4 tablespoons fresh or dried coconut shavings
75 g (3 oz) stem ginger in syrup, drained and thinly sliced

2 egg yolks
50 g (2 oz) caster sugar
grated rind of 1 lime
50 ml (2 fl oz) white wine
4 tablespoons crème fraîche

1 Arrange the pineapple slices well spaced apart on a large heatproof platter. Scatter over the coconut shavings and slices of ginger.

2 Place the egg yolks and sugar in a large heatproof bowl and set over a pan of simmering water, ensuring that the water is not touching the bottom of the bowl (it could scramble the egg). Using an electric beater beat the mixture for about 5 minutes until well combined, frothy and slightly thickened. Pour in the lime juice and wine and beat again until smooth and well thickened.

3 Pre-heat the grill to high. Gradually stir the crème fraîche into the egg-yolk mixture and whisk for another 3 minutes until well combined. Spoon the sabayon over the pineapple and place under the hot grill for a couple of minutes until golden. Serve immediately.

# Bottoms up!

# Drinks

Brilliant bloody marys • The ultimate irish coffee • apple and mint vodka • Peach bellini • Honey and vanilla-bean smoothie

Nutrition notes per serving:
calories 86
protein 1 g
carbohydrate 5 g
fat none
saturated fat none
fibre 0.8 g
added sugar 4 g
salt 1.37 g

# Brilliant bloody marys

I've found the best Bloody Marys are achieved with tomato juice from a can, as it is much thinner than tomato juice from cartons, no matter how expensive they are. The horseradish is an optional extra, but it gives an excellent kick.

Preparation time: 5 minutes • Cooking time: none • Serves 6–8

an 800 g (1 lb 8 oz) can tomato juice
1–2 tablespoons Worcestershire sauce
½–1 teaspoon Tabasco sauce
1–1½ teaspoons celery salt
juice of 1–2 limes

2 teaspoons grated fresh horseradish
 (optional)
about 175 g (6 oz) crushed ice
150 ml (¼ pint) vodka
50 ml (2 fl oz) dry fino sherry

1 Place the tomato juice in a large cocktail shaker with 1 tablespoon of the Worcestershire sauce, half a teaspoon of Tabasco, 1 teaspoon of celery salt, the juice of 1 lime and the grated fresh horseradish, if using. Fill up with some of the ice and shake until well chilled. Add the vodka and sherry, and then shake again. Taste and adjust seasoning as necessary. Strain into tall, sturdy glasses, top with the remaining ice and serve.

This recipe makes about 1.2 litres (2 pints), so if you don't have a large enough cocktail shaker you'll need to shake it in two batches.

# The ultimate irish coffee

Nutrition notes per serving:
calories 377
protein 1 g
carbohydrate 26 g
fat 23 g
saturated fat 13 g
fibre none
added sugar 24 g
salt 0.08 g

A little indulgence is a wonderful thing and it doesn't come much better than this – a luxurious Irish coffee with a couple of extra shots of liqueur, topped with cream. They say it's best to use warm glasses – I just run them under a hot tap.

Preparation time: 5 minutes • Cooking time: 10 minutes • Serves 2

85 ml (3 fl oz) double cream, well chilled
2 tablespoons sugar
2 tablespoons Irish whiskey
2 tablespoons Baileys

2 tablespoons Kahlúa (coffee liqueur)
300 ml (½ pint) freshly brewed, piping hot espresso coffee
a pinch of freshly grated nutmeg

1 Heat a small, heavy-based frying-pan over a medium heat. Place the cream in a bowl and lightly whip, then chill until needed. Sprinkle the sugar over the base of the frying-pan and allow to caramelize, without stirring. Pour in the whiskey and quickly flambé, then stir in the Baileys and Kahlúa and gently heat for about a minute until smooth, stirring occasionally. Divide between glasses then pour in the coffee, stirring to combine. Carefully pour a layer of cream on top of each one, over the back of a spoon. Add a tiny grating of nutmeg and serve at once.

You could warm the glasses the traditional Irish way, using an old-fashioned spirit lamp, but I don't suppose many of you will have one to hand …

Nutrition notes per serving:
  calories 194
  protein 0.3 g
  carbohydrate 33 g
  fat 0.1 g
  saturated fat none
  fibre 1 g
  added sugar 4 g
  salt 0.03 g

# Apple and mint vodka

This is a refreshing summer-time drink, but don't get too carried away – although it is very easy to drink, it is actually very potent! You may need to alter the amount of sugar you use depending on how sweet the apples are.

Preparation time: 10 minutes • Cooking time: none • Serves 4

a small bunch of fresh mint
2 Granny Smith apples, quartered, cored
  and chopped
1 tablespoon sugar

120 ml (4 fl oz) vodka
about 175 g (6 oz) ice cubes
1 litre (2 pints) tonic or soda water

1  Set aside 4 mint sprigs to use as a garnish, then strip the remaining leaves from the stalks and place in either a cocktail shaker or a tall, sturdy jug. Add the apple pieces and sugar, then smash together to form a lumpy pulp, using the end of a rolling pin. Pour in the vodka and fill up with ice. Shake or stir until very well chilled.

2  Half-fill tall glasses with fresh ice cubes and strain over the chilled vodka mixture, then top up with tonic or soda water. Decorate with the reserved mint sprigs to serve.

You could use any variety of dessert apple in this recipe, but I prefer the sharpness of a good old Granny Smith.

If you want to be posh, use a piece of peach to wipe around the rim of each glass, then dip the tops of the glasses in a saucer of caster sugar for a frosted effect.

# Peach bellini

This drink originates from Harry's Bar in Venice where the peaches are chopped by hand in front of you. They may disapprove, but I find that a can of drained peaches in natural juice works just as well when fresh peaches are unavailable.

Nutrition notes per serving:
calories 122
protein 1 g
carbohydrate 14 g
fat 0.1 g
saturated fat none
fibre 1 g
added sugar 4 g
salt 0.01 g

Preparation time: 5 minutes • Cooking time: none • Serves 4

2 large, ripe peaches
1 tablespoon caster sugar
2 tablespoons brandy

375 ml (13 fl oz) Champagne or
    sparkling wine, well chilled (about
    ½ a bottle)

1 Peel the peaches using a vegetable peeler and then cut in half, remove the stones and cut into slices.

2 Place the peach slices in a food processor or liquidizer with the sugar and brandy, then blend until smooth. Pour into a small jug and chill until ready to use.

3 Divide the peach purée between Champagne flutes or long-stemmed glasses and top up with the Champagne or sparkling wine. Serve immediately.

# low fat! Honey and vanilla-bean smoothie

Pure vanilla-bean paste can be found in jars from the special selection or gourmet food section of large supermarkets. It is basically the same as scraping out the seeds from inside a vanilla pod, but easier and with far less waste.

Preparation time: 5 minutes • Cooking time: none • Serves 4

450 ml (¾ pint) milk, well chilled
150 ml (¼ pint) thick Greek yoghurt, well chilled
2–3 tablespoons clear honey

2 tablespoons pure vanilla-bean paste (or the scraped-out seeds from 2 vanilla pods)
about 175 g (6 oz) ice cubes

1 Blend the milk, yoghurt, 2 tablespoons of the honey and the vanilla paste in a food processor or liquidizer with a handful of the ice cubes until smooth. Taste and add a little more honey if necessary. Fill tall glasses half full with ice and then top with the smoothie. Serve at once.

**VARIATIONS**
**Banana smoothie:** add 2 peeled, chopped bananas and reduce the honey by one tablespoon.
**Berry smoothie:** add 150 g (5 oz) of fresh or frozen mixed berries.
**Amaretto smoothie:** replace the vanilla-bean paste with 5 tablespoons of Amaretto liqueur.

# Menus

Why not have a go at some of these tasty menu suggestions?

## Low-fat feast

This menu is full of clean, fresh flavours. It's such a delicious combination that no one will ever guess it's low in fat.

Pomegranate, orange and mint salad

Lemongrass and lime fish stew

Pineapple, ginger and coconut sabayon

## Cook-ahead supper

There are often times when you want to serve a delicious supper but you know you're going to be short of time. This menu is the answer to your prayers as it can all be prepared the day before. The soup can just be reheated and served while the pies are cooking in the oven.

Beetroot borscht

Tempting turkey, leek and mushroom pies

Coconut carrot cake with rosemary cream

# Having a party – oriental style!

This menu should easily serve 8 people (with some leftovers). I would serve the main course with a big bowl of fragrant rice.

Honey-glazed duck with sticky rice

Wok-style pak choi

Stir-fried ginger pork with squeaky greens

Sirloin skewers with sweet peppers and shiitake

Warm mascarpone berry spring rolls (double quantity)

# Summer sunshine lunch

This is a nice, light combination of dishes and should leave you with plenty of room for the Dreamy chocolate hazelnut torte. I like to serve the torte with fresh summer berries and a dollop of crème fraîche.

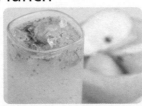

Apple and mint vodka

Sweet chilli tomato tarte tatin

Mustard-salmon, avocado and watercress salad

Dreamy chocolate hazelnut torte

# The morning after the night before

Prepare as much of this menu as you can the day before. The seasoned tomato juice for the Bloody marys and the Banana tarte tatin can be prepared ahead ... then all you have to do is sit back and take the compliments!

Brilliant bloody marys

Huevos rancheros

Banana tarte tatin

# Veggie delight

For many meat eaters entertaining veggies can be a bit daunting. But I guarantee you can't go wrong with this fab menu; it's sure to be a hit.

Roasted balsamic beetroot

Penne pecorino and broad bean gratin

Coconut carrot cake with rosemary cream

# Stars and stripes supper

I love an excuse for a party, so why not take a lesson from our friends across the Atlantic and celebrate Thanksgiving? This menu is packed with American style.

Maryland crab cakes with caper salsa

Pan-fried chicken with corncakes

Double chocolate croissant pudding with bourbon

## The ultimate comfort food

There are times in everyone's life when you just want some comfort food. It might be freezing outside or you just want to cheer someone up; maybe it's a Sunday night and it's your last treat before another dreary Monday morning.

Pukka pea soup with crispy bacon crème fraîche

Fabulous fish pies with prawns

Clare's chocolate, coffee and cardamom mousse

## Time for the footie

I always have my mates round when there's a big game on – and sometimes I even feed them. Serve these dishes all at once, or at intervals throughout the match.

Chickpea and chorizo fritters

Sweet eddie cajun wedges

Jimmy's chicken chompers

## Something for the kids

The Sausage and pea risotto is just perfect for kids ... and they're sure to enjoy helping you prepare the Eton mess with maddie maltesers.

Sausage and pea risotto

Eton mess with maddie maltesers

## Festive feast

This menu is perfect for Christmas Eve when all the family get together, or you could increase the quantities and serve it at a New Year's Eve party. Add any leftover Christmas fruit and nuts to the couscous – it will taste even more fab.

Beetroot salad with basil and lemon croutons

Lamb tagine with minted, herbed couscous

Orange-flower, yoghurt and pistachio pudding

## Christmas hamper

For me, there's nothing nicer than receiving a gift that someone has gone to the trouble of making themselves. There are a number of recipes in the book that would be suitable to give as a gift, in a hamper, or just on their own. Buy some attractive jars and make your own hand-written labels, giving a couple of serving suggestions on the back of each pot.

Onion marmalade

Aubergine chutney

Walnut and herb pesto

Chilli ginger jam

Chilli and herb cajun cornbread

Coconut carrot cake with rosemary cream

Sour cream and chive muffins (or a variation)

## Let's celebrate!

If you've got a reason to celebrate, then this is the perfect menu for you. The Peach bellinis will get the party off to a great start, and who could resist my Roquefort and walnut soufflés? Mmm!

Peach bellini

Roquefort and walnut soufflés

Venison steaks with stewed plums and garlic mash

Banana tarte tatin

## Lazy sunday lunch

This lunch can be prepared in under an hour ... and no one will be any the wiser!

Mushroom, almond and garlic soup

Pan-roasted pork with white bean purée

Easy baileys crème brûlée

The ultimate irish coffee

# Index

Page numbers in **bold** indicate recipes. Page numbers in *italics* refer to illustrations.

# Acknowledgements

It's always difficult to know where to start when it comes to acknowledgements. There are those, of course, who are directly involved, but we can't forget the talent that makes my job of cooking so much easier. So cheers Gary the butcher, Joe in the deli, and numerous friendly faces at my local supermarket … and not forgetting Ahmed, my trusty mini-cab driver. May the back window be fixed sometime soon!

It was once again a great pleasure to work with Orla Broderick, who stimulates my culinary brain and agrees with me that food should be unfussy, the best you can afford and should always essentially be a pleasure to eat and to share. Thanks to Bethany Heald, for her energy, enthusiasm and attention to detail in the studio. (Hope the flat is a great success.) To Howard Shooter for creating the sensiferous photographs which accompany the recipes in my book. To Rachel Copus, my gentle-voiced editor, who keeps me focussed even when Arsenal lose (not that often, thankfully!) and a host of others at BBC books, including Nicky Ross, my commissioning editor – thanks for keeping Meals in Minutes alive – and the team, Sarah, Susannah and Malika, who really know how to make books that people enjoy.

To my agents Jeremy 'Chelski' Hicks and Sarah Dalkin, who have denied me the famous agent-client tension by being endlessly supportive and all-round good people. I love you too, J.D.

To Clare and the kids, Jimmy and Maddie, without whom I could not find the motivation and inspiration to smile continuously, even when the soufflé flops (Sorry Clare)! And to my dog, Oscar Poska, for those lovely walks when I'm feeling brain–dead.